A HISTORY OF CAMBRIDGESHIRE

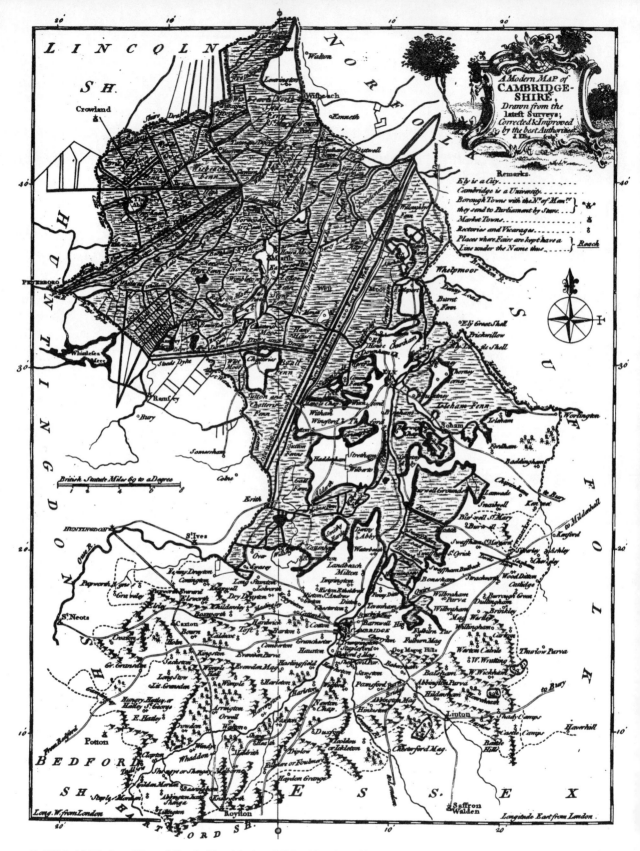

J. Ellis's 'A Modern Map of Cambridgeshire', published in 1766 (from a copy in the Cambridgeshire Collection)

THE DARWEN COUNTY HISTORY SERIES

A History of Cambridgeshire

BRUCE GALLOWAY

Illustrations from the Cambridgeshire Collection

Cartography by Janet Kershaw

PHILLIMORE

1983

Published by
PHILLIMORE & CO. LTD.
Shopwyke Hall, Chichester, Sussex

ISBN 0 85033 450 0

Printed in Great Britain by
BIDDLES LTD.
Guildford, Surrey

and bound by
THE NEWDIGATE PRESS LTD.
Dorking, Surrey

Contents

List of Plates

Maps

Preface and Acknowledgements

All books are a co-operative enterprise, and this one is no exception. It relies on the work of a hundred and more scholars, living and dead; of all the people who staff Cambridgeshire's libraries and museums; and of my publishers. To all of these, I give my thanks.

A special debt of gratitude is, however, owed to the following—

(a) Mike Petty and the staff of the Cambridgeshire Collection, for their indefatigable help, interest and courtesy at all times. This book could certainly not have been written without them.

(b) The Cambridge Antiquarian Society, whose *Proceedings* are such an invaluable source of material for the local historian.

(c) David Hall, the Fenland Archaeological Officer, for his advice and assistance in the early part of the project.

(d) Tony Claydon, for his excellent line drawings.

(e) Verity Galloway, for her support early in the project and in typing part of the manuscript.

(f) Exeter University, for providing me with travel expenses during the last hectic months of writing and cross-checking.

In the classic author's phrase, the book is the better for their help, the mistakes are mine alone. I hope it will serve at least as an introduction to the fascinating history of the old county of Cambridgeshire and the Isle of Ely and encourage others to produce a more complete volume.

BRUCE GALLOWAY
1983

I Before the Romans

Introduction

If you leave Cambridge on the A.603, turn off at Barton down the 'B' road signposted to St Neots and keep going for five miles, through Comberton and Toft, you come to the village of Kingston, on the western border of the old county of Cambridgeshire. Leave your car by the church and walk south down the main street to the sharp bend left up Claypit Hill. At this point a broad green lane takes off south-west towards Eversden Wood. (The track can be wet and rutted even in the driest months: it is best tackled in a drought, or on a winter morning when the frost lies on the ground.) After a long mile the path ends in a crossing road by New Farm. Turn east here. Ignore the next corner and plunge into the shelter-belt of woodland down an inviting bridlepath. You soon leave the trees behind and emerge on to the top of broad, rolling arable land which falls away on either side. This is the Mare Way.

This short journey will have taken you successively through every period of the county's history. The road on which you left Cambridge is Akeman Street, constructed by the Romans. The villages through which you passed have the characteristic '-ton' place-names of the Anglo-Saxons (save for 'Toft', a Danish word). In medieval and Tudor times, Kingston was an important market town and it retains a fine church with its own wall-paintings and many delightful thatched cottages from those centuries. The woodland belt through which you walked shelter the estate of Wimpole Hall, Cambridgeshire's finest country mansion, dating from the 17th and 18th centuries. The fields to your left and right were enclosed after the Napoleonic Wars. Looking north, a metallic glint in the valley can be identified as the radio telescope at Barton, bringing us into our own times and, arguably, those still to come. The only period not mentioned is the pre-Roman, and that lies under your feet.

The Mare Way is one of the oldest identified tracks in Cambridge-shire. It enters the county a mile or so from where you join it and snakes along the hilltops between two lines of later villages—through the Eversdens, Harlton and Haslingfield to the north, and through Orwell and Barrington to the south. It is indeed a prehistoric 'ridgeway'. The way at one point reaches a height of 250ft. above sea level, but soon slopes gently down to 200ft. above Haslingfield. From there, it

The Geographical and Geological divisions of the County.

descends abruptly through fields to ford the Cam at Harston Mill—one of the most important prehistoric river crossings, which has yielded finds from every age before the Romans. The feeling of height is enormous. So is the view. From Chapel Hill you can see the hills beyond Royston and 200 parishes of the county, and on a clear day as far as Ely. Today, the scene is a patchwork of farmland, which shows how greatly man has developed the countryside. The prehistoric traveller would have faced quite a different panorama.

Cambridgeshire's natural geographic divisions are well-defined. In the north are the fens. The only 'high' lying ground here is on the 'islands' of clay, like Ely, March, and Chatteris. Between lie the flatlands—enormous black fields of peat, either fertile or flooded, and separated by a maze of drains. In the far north is a strip of silt fen around Wisbech, which is firmer, marginally higher ground, deposited by marine flooding. To the south are the uplands—so called, though never rising over 400ft. above sea level. In the west and far south-east are hilly areas covered in boulder clay—the same clay, deposited by ice sheets, that covers the North Essex Highlands immediately south of Cambridgeshire. Between these clay plateaux lies a belt of open chalkland crossing the county from south-west to north-east, which was of great importance in prehistoric times. Chalk and clay alike are fissured by the river valleys of the Cam and its tributaries, each laying down a strip of alluvial soil.

What did this landscape look like during prehistoric times? Unfortunately great physical changes due to climate, land subsidence and the activities of man make it difficult for us to imagine. However, in the upland areas throughout this period the claylands were forested with oak, elm, ash, and dense undergrowth, which would have been forbidding to settlers with primitive tools, and so only isolated pockets of settlement occurred here. The primary area of occupation lay on the lighter soils and the natural lines of communication, such as the river valleys and the chalk belt. The valleys of the Ashwell, Saffron Walden and Linton Cam contain a wealth of prehistoric material. So does the chalk strip which forms part of a much larger belt of chalkland trade and settlement, linking the two most populated areas in prehistoric Britain—Wiltshire and the Brecklands. The tracks connecting these are often called the Icknield Way. It is, however, wrong to see this as a single, continuous highway. The chalk runs south-west and is often only a few miles wide. Instead there was a line of settlements, linked to each other by local paths following the direction of the chalk. The result was a mass of parallel tracks over dry, easily-traversable country from which light woodland had been cleared. This was not, however, the most fertile land for arable farming. That lay on the northern edge

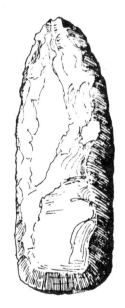

Early Neolithic scraper, with polished edge

of the belt, especially east of Cambridge, where the dry, infertile chalk meets the fertile but treacherous peatlands of the southern fens.

The fenlands present a more varied picture, dependent upon sea levels. At the beginning of this period the fens lay comfortably above the waves, the coastline receding as far north and east as the Dogger Bank. The land quickly became wooded, at first with birch and pine, though later with the denser oak forests. The arrival of wetter conditions after 3000 B.C. drastically disturbed this situation. Rivers flooded and became meres, rotting trees and scrub became peat, and isolated the fen islands. Marine incursions and the tilting of Britain from west to east deposited silt in the north, overlying the peat. There were brief periods of recovery, for example in the Bronze Age, but by the end of this period fenland had become almost entirely uninhabitable.

The Age of Stone (10,000–2000 B.C.)

There is an enormous difference between the first men in Cambridgeshire and those who faced the bronze-bearing Beaker People. Even to talk of 'Stone Age Man' obscures the greater size, sophistication and permanence of Neolithic than of Palaeolithic settlement.

Bone fish-spear prong from Royston

Indeed, it is misleading to refer to 'settlement' at all in the Old and Middle Stone Ages. No hut sites remain from this period. The whole county can boast only two floors on which flints were worked. Men and women were nomadic hunters and gatherers, who formed small groups to follow the game on which they lived. Their diet was mixed with nuts, berries and herbs. They may have put up crude wattle shelters to give them some protection at night. Certainly they used fire, made clothes, and later tents from animal skins, and created a variety of weapons. The most popular was the hand-axe, formed from a flint block by repeated blows of another flint hammer. Such axes have been found on several fen islands, in the Granta Valley, at Kennett, Swaffham Bulbeck, and near the Cambridge–Girton road. Mesolithic man developed more sophisticated weapons which could be used over long distances, such as bows and arrows tipped with tiny flaked flints, and a remarkable bone fish-spear from Royston. Smaller flakes were used as scrapers and borers, especially for leatherwork. Their existence was precarious, dependent upon climate and the movement of beasts.

The last 1,000 years of this period, the Neolithic or New Stone Age, saw a dramatic change in the human condition, visible in its archaeological remains. The range of flints increased enormously. The Cambridge Museum of Archaeology and Ethnology contains chipped gouges, picks, awls, scrapers, and fabricators; leaf-shaped, tanged, winged, and

14

barbed arrows; chipped and polished discs; and a grinding-slab from Burwell on which polished flints were produced. Mass-mining had begun at Grime's Graves in the Brecklands, and many of the flints came from that remarkable place. Flints, bone and wood, were now, however, only part of man's working material. Semi-precious stones like jadeite were used for axes, and Baltic amber was made into beads. There is evidence of woollen textiles and pottery. Early pots were extremely crude, built up by hands in coils and fired in domestic hearths. Finds come predominantly from the 'primary area of occupation'—the river valleys, fen edge, and island. There is the first evidence of settlement, in huts with turf walls, a framework of posts and stakes, and an entrance covered with skins. Important dead were buried in long barrows, like that on Therfield Down (*see* Plate 1). Sometimes Neolithic man built causewayed camps and ceremonial meeting sites (*henges*)—possibly ones in Cambridgeshire being at Melbourn and Wilbraham.

Neolithic flint arrowhead from Chatteris

This explosion of activity was based on the economic valuation of agriculture. Domestic animal remains in Neolithic settlements show that a semi-nomadic, mixed pastoral and hunting economy had evolved by 2500 B.C., with goats, sheep and cattle providing milk and meat. For the first time, people could congregate in sufficient numbers with sufficient leisure to create things that nowadays we take for granted. It was scarcely an easy life, but marked an enormous advance on previous times.

The Age of Bronze (2000–600 B.C.)

The arrival of metal objects did not immediately revolutionise prehistoric life and traditional tools and lifestyles remained very important.

Similarities between early Bronze Age man and his predecessors were many. He settled in the same river valleys, chalklands, fen edge, and islands. A drier climate permitted some incursions into the peat fens, and three timber causeways were built to Ely. One favourite technique was transhumance grazing of cattle on fenland during the summer months, and on the chalk belt in winter. Farming remained pastoral, though progressively more settled, and was supplemented by the hunting of deer, fishing and gathering—notably of wild grains such as barley and wheat. The tumulus remained the burial place for important persons, but instead of the single long barrow on the borders of the county, scores of round barrows with many different designs—discs, wheels, bells, etc.—were used. These are clustered in definite groups, mostly along the Icknield Way, the most notable ones being

Socketed celt from Burwell Fen

15

on Thriplow Heath, the Fleam Dyke, at Wilbraham, Snailwell, and Chippenham. Barrows at Snailwell yielded 52 separate interments and one tumulus was over 60ft. across. Skeletons of ponies found here suggest a continuing nomadic tradition, and other animal bones indicate funeral feasts or ritual slaughtering to feed the spirit on its travels to an 'Otherworld'. Cremation was the rule, and the ashes were placed in cinerary urns with thick rims. Other pottery objects found include a rustic 'beer-mug' with a dartboard design on its base. These vessels were introduced to Cambridgeshire by the Beaker People, a tall, round-headed race that entered the county from the Wash and spread down the chalk belt. Pottery aside, their distinctive achievements were in the exquisite refinement of their flint daggers, arrowheads and other tools. In this early period (before 1600 B.C.), metal goods were rare, limited to the occasional knife or flat-axe.

A Beaker Period 'beer mug'

The Middle Bronze Age (1500–1000 B.C.) was a period of comparative prosperity, with an extensive trade in luxury objects: jet from Yorkshire; amber from the Baltic; and gold. The most splendid of all prehistoric finds was made in 1844 in Grunty Fen by a labourer digging turf for fuel: he found a pure gold torc weighing 5oz., 4ft. long around the curves, which was made by twisting together two gummed ribbons of gold into a single strand, and was probably Irish in manufacture. In neighbouring areas were found these three characteristic weapons of the age: the palstave, looped spearhead, and rapier, beautifully made.

The Late Bronze Age (1000–600 B.C.) saw further changes in lifestyle. An inexorable climatic deterioration turned peat fens to marsh, driving settlers back to the fen edge and islands. The construction of round barrows declined and was replaced by inhumation in flat graves. Trade and technology continued to advance. The number and quality of worked flints declined rapidly, in the face of bronze. The palstave gave way to the hollow-cast socketed axe, the looped to the riveted spearhead, the rapier to the leaf-shaped sword. Shields found at Coveney and Chatteris indicate that sheet metal could be hammered to an even thickness. Designs show the influence of the Continent, and of south-west England. Trade reached new levels, itinerant smith-merchants burying hoards of bronze for reworking. By 600 B.C. the inhabitants were a settled, pastoral people, evenly spread throughout the primary area of occupation. The contrast with the nomadic herders of the Neolithic period is very clear.

The Age of Iron (600 B.C.–A.D. 43)

In the 6th century B.C. Britain again became subject to a wave of settlement. Like the Beaker People, these foreigners brought an exciting new technology: the use of iron.

1. An aerial view of Therfield Down near Royston shows a Neolithic long barrow and several Bronze Age round barrows. The Icknield Way passes the Downs to the north.

2. On of the remaining Romano-British burial mounds on Bartlow known simply as 'The Hills'. Rich finds excavated here were destroyed in a fire at Easton Lodge, in 1847.

3. Looking north-west up the Roman canal of Reach Lode, towards Wicken Fen. Roman remains have been found scattered along its banks.

4. Flean Dyke: a look along the *vallum* with the ditch falling away to the left. This is one of four defensive earthworks connecting fen and forest, probably constructed in the 7th century by the Kingdom of East Anglia.

Iron is in many ways inferior to bronze as it is a soft, brittle metal. An invading warrior using his iron sword on the bronze shield from Coveney might have spent 10 minutes hammering it flat again afterwards! It was, however, cheaper, more readily available, and easier to work. Iron objects became common not merely in the trappings of court and battle, but in the everyday use of richer households. In addition to swords, shields and brooches, buckles, pins, fire-dogs, chains and ploughshares were worked in iron. More intensive arable agriculture became possible. Population increased, and settlements ate into the primeval forests of the clay interior. At the end of the period we see the first evidence of some form of political organisation: tribes were bonded into 'nations', kings issued coinage, and orders were sent out from recognised 'capitals'. Trade flourished, serving these 'cities'.

It is therefore disappointing that the early evidence from Cambridgeshire is so minimal. There are a few burials, flat graves or secondary interments in round barrows, yielding characteristic skeletons and meagre grave goods. Some early homestead sites have been discovered, mostly beneath later settlements and hill-forts. That is all.

The newcomers were Brythonic Celts—a tall, long-headed people from northern Europe, entering the county down the Wash and the Suffolk-Essex river valleys. They settled predictably away from forest and flooded fen. An early site at Linton is unusual for its size and rectangular shape. At this state, people slept in extended family groups; later sites show numerous small circular houses for man, woman and child. Houses were constructed of wattle and daub, the walls and thatched reed roof were supported upon a framework of posts. Objects found at Linton include bone needles and combs, a clay spindle-whorl, gouges and leather-working tools, pins, and characteristically East Anglian coarse pottery, hand-made with finger-tip ornament and applied bands. Some wide-mouthed bowls with angular shoulders resemble finds in Berkshire and Wiltshire. Other early settlements were at Abington Piggotts, Grantchester, Trumpington, Haslingfield, Barrington, Stuntney and Hauxton Mill. The only weapon discovered from this period is an iron spearhead from a warrior's burial at Soham. More elaborate finds come from Newnham Croft, and include bangles, bosses and rings as well as a fine bronze brooch.

Few possessed such elegant adornments. Most were peasants, tilling small square fields and pasturing their animals. The most important settlements were in forts like Wandlebury and the Cherry Hinton War Ditches. Excavations there indicate fortification in the 3rd century B.C. and suggest a hierarchical, military society with a warrior aristocracy.

Bronze Age spear-end from Burwell

17

They were soon dispossessed by an incursion of Belgic Celts who pressed northward through Gaul by Roman expansion, *c*. 70 B.C., a systematic invasion of southern Britain, driving the Brythons north and west. The main tribes in eastern England were the Catuvellauni and Trinovantes—described by Caesar as an aggressive people, who fought from chariots. During this period in Cambridgeshire there was frantic construction of defences by the native Brythonic Iceni—at Barrington, Arbury Camps, Willingham (Belsar's Hill), and Fowlmere, where the Round Moats included water from a diverted brook.

Wandlebury is a particularly interesting site. It is in a commanding position on the crest of the Gogmagog Hills, overlooking the ford at

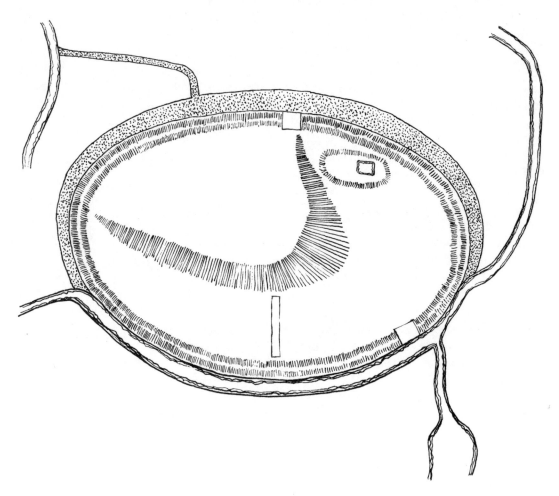

Round Moats. A plan of the Round Moats at Fowlmere showing the banked enclosures, ditch, current watercourses and silted-up moat on the E (top) side.

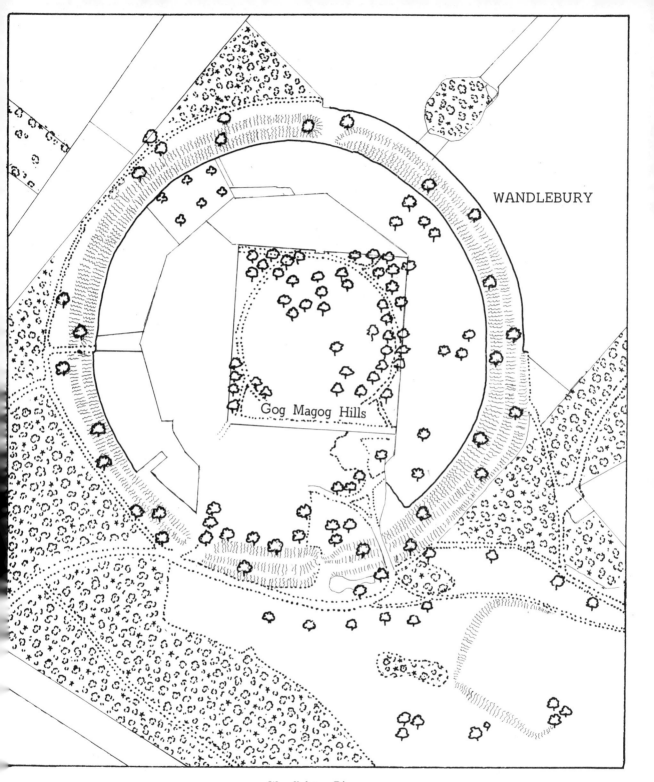

WANDLEBURY

Gog Magog Hills

Wandlebury Ring

19

Cambridge, guarding the Cam valley and flanking the chalk belt tracks. Surviving defences scarcely look impenetrable: a single ditch 8ft. deep, bounded by an exterior bank 5ft. high and an interior 2ft. high, surrounding a circular enclosure 1,000ft. across containing houses and wooded gardens. The Earl of Godolphin constructed a shooting-box here in the 18th century, thereby destroying an inner rampart and ditch in the process. This unwittingly restored the earliest Iron Age fort, the single-ditched enclosure built before the Belgic invasion. The triumphant Belgae had dug a further ditch and rampart, topped possibly with wooden palisades. Their victory at nearby War Ditches is marked by the scattered bodies of dead Iceni. Tribal wars continued until the Roman invasion, and the Iceni were pushed north into the fens and east into East Anglia. One casualty was a Catuvellaunian chieftain, buried at Snailwell about A.D. 30. He was buried on a wooded couch with lavish trimmings: including a platter; a bronze bowl; a superb spiral armlet over 3ft. long, with duck's head terminals; a shield; and leather armour. A feast was held beside the grave, including four large jugs (*amphorae*) of Gaulish wine. These were ritually smashed, tipped into the grave, and the whole set alight.

Belgic remains are as numerous as Brythonic were few. The Snailwell chieftain was the archetypal warrior-aristocrat. The wine jugs confirm a wealth of evidence showing links with the Continent. The Catuvellauni imported wine, oil and luxury goods, exporting grain, cattle and slaves, including Iceni captured in war. Like other Belgic tribes, however, they were capable of fine workmanship, especially in metal and pottery. The first wheel-thrown pots are from this period—graceful pedestalled vases, barrel-shaped urns, fine bowls and beakers. They had their own coinage, crude copies of Greek Philippics bearing the names Tascioranus and Cunobelinus. Elaborate household goods like fire-dogs, pot-boilers, cooking vessels, water-clocks, rings, torcs, and enamelled brooches were made, along with a mass of combs, spindle-whorls, horse-trappings, buckets and seal-boxes. Settlements again were sited along the rivers, the fen edge and the chalk belt, and a number of cemeteries or urnfields containing cremated bodies have been found.

Their beliefs are uncertain. Evidence of druidic worship in Cambridgeshire is non-existent, though decapitated female bodies in a cemetery at Guilden Morden may indicate belief in witchcraft. For more formal religion, we must return to Wandlebury.

> If a warrior enters this level space at the dead of night, when the moon is shining, and cries, 'Knight to knight, come forth', immediately he will be confronted by a warrior, armed for the fight who, charging horse to horse, either dismounts his adversary or is dismounted.

The author was the 13th-century Romancer, Gervase of Tilbury. It is one of many legends about the fort. Local traditions speak of a golden chariot buried there, and a giant chalk figure in the turf. The antiquary William Cole refers to this figure in the 18th century, as still visible and related it to the biblical giant, Gogmagog. In 1954, T. C. Lethbridge decided to find the giant, using a 'depth-sounding' technique with a heavy bar used by West Country farmers to identify blocked drains. A figure appeared, identified as a breasted goddess with a white horse. This he labelled Epona, a Celtic fertility goddess worshipped by the (matriarchal) Iceni. Other figures were 'discovered': a chariot; a sun god with wings; a crescent moon over Epona; a giant warrior wielding an enormous sword. Like the goddess, these were cut in flowing, Celtic lines, but had a more direct, 'naturalistic' air. Lethbridge considered them additions by the patriarchal Catuvellauni after their take-over to create a scene from their own religion: the Moon Goddess in her chariot being rescued by her husband the Sun God from the Dark Warrior of the Night—a portrayal of dawn.

Scholars almost unanimously rejected Lethbridge, and it is easy to see why. The size and complexity of the designs far exceeded any other chalk figures in this country. Stylistic similarities with the Cerne Giant and the White Horse of Uffington were explained away, as was the presence of Roman pottery and Celtic slingstones in hollows within the figure. Glacial action was suggested, and the technique of bar-sounding criticised. Lethbridge countered such accusations vigorously, but had little support. Today only a bumpy hillside beside the main path up to the Ring survives to testify to Lethbridge's work. The face, chest and breast of 'Epona' are all visible—but were they there 2,000 years ago, or only since excavation?

A drawing of the chalk figures proposed by Lethbridge after his excavation. Epona the Celtic Goddess, is clearly visible in the centre. The Sun God (L), Dark Warrior (R) and Golden Chariot with horse make up the rest of the design.

II Under the Eagles

The Conquest

*Early Romano-British
and Imperial coinage*

The pattern of life in Roman Cambridgeshire is clear, from a mass of archaeological finds, but all the major historical events of the time took place infuriatingly across the borders—in Essex, Huntingdonshire, Peterborough, and the Brecklands. This is unsurprising. The county was in A.D. 43 a frontier area, disputed between tribes. The Roman conquest bypassed the district. The Catuvellauni to the west resisted the advance of the legions and were defeated; the Iceni hurriedly made peace, and were rewarded with autonomy by Rome. The legions then pushed north through Huntingdonshire and the Soke, planting a fort at Godmanchester and garrisons at Longthorpe and Water Newton on the Nene. In the next four years they extended control throughout southern Britain and began to tackle the Welsh tribes under Caratacus. Only at that point did Roman troops come into action in Cambridgeshire. Governor Scapula's order disarming all Britons was resisted by some fenland Iceni, and enforced by a punitive assault from Longthorpe on their fortified camp at Stonea. It was a small foretaste of things to come.

In A.D. 60, Prasutagus of the Iceni died, leaving as joint heirs his wife, Boudicca, and the Emperor of Rome. Subsequent events are uncertain. The Iceni permitted female inheritance—the Romans did not. Legionaries entered the capital to enforce the imperial interests and took over the kingdom and allegedly raped the queen. The Iceni rebelled. Boudicca's revolt swept through the county, and a force from Longthorpe under Petillius Cerealis was annihilated and the fort destroyed. The Trinovantes then revolted, overwhelming the veteran colony imposed on them. London and *Verulamium* (St Albans) were sacked before the return of Suetonius from Wales faced them with battle—and defeat. The Roman revenge was merciless. Iceni coin hoards at Wisbech, Wimblington, and March indicate that frantic attempts were made to secure wealth in the face of legionary advance. Settlements were razed, populations enslaved, and new forts constructed at Cambridge and Great Chesterford. The tribal capital was forcibly moved to *Venta*, near Norwich, and autonomy removed. The region thus became part of Roman *Britannia*. It was the end of independence for this region, as for the entire province. It was the beginning of a long peace.

Roman slave shackles

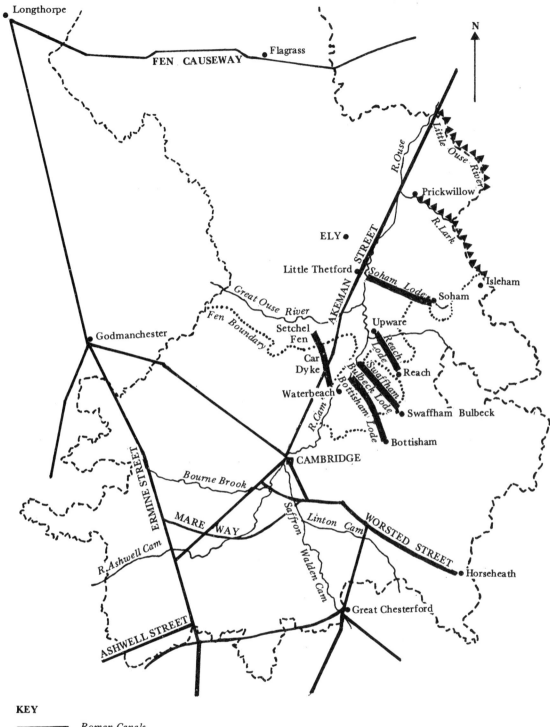

Roman Roads and Canals

Centuries of Construction

The following three centuries were years of peace and prosperity for the province. It was a period of great civil constructions, bringing city life to Cambridgeshire. Roads and canals were built and the fens were drained.

The most lasting part of this construction was the roads. Their original function was military, to allow speedy passage of soldiers between centres of war. Quickly, they became arteries of commerce and travel also. The map shows their distribution throughout the county. The most famous was Ermine Street, the military highway from London to Lincoln and York. This passes through western Cambridgeshire between Royston and Caxton Gibbet, *en route* to Godmanchester and Water Newton. Akeman Street and Worstead Street were the two other principal upland routes. The former connected Ermine Street to Cambridge, Ely and the fens, and Worstead Street linked Godmanchester to Cambridge and Cambridge to the Colne valley. Worstead Street was never completed beyond Horseheath, but its original destination was probably *Camulodunum* (Colchester). It was built from the Cambridge end, on the low ridge above the populated Granta valley. Its construction was typical: a bed of natural chalk covered with a layer of rammed chalk and a rounded topping of good coarse gravel, with drainage ditches to either side. A spur connected the street to the camp of Great Chesterford, at the Icknield Way crossing. The Icknield, like the Mare's Way, remained of the greatest commercial importance. Both were partially Romanised, Ashwell Street in the south-west being surfaced and straightened west of Ermine Street. In the far north, fen causeways carried a road from Water Newton and Peterborough through Flaggrass to Denver—possibly *en route* for the Peddar's Way. These roads drove straight through open tracts of country, generally ignoring belts of occupation served by existing routes. Inevitably, however, settlements developed beside the roads. 'Way stations' existed at Arrington Bridge on Ermine Street and at Horseheath. The most important towns lay on road junctions. Great Chesterford in Essex was a walled town of 35 acres, with a large cemetery. Godmanchester and Water Newton (*Durobrivae*) were military as well as civil centres, guarding river crossings on Ermine Street. They were the commercial, administrative and judicial centres for the surrounding countryside; the provincial market through which goods manufactured in the major cities reached the villas; and where proclamations were read and justice done.

Cambridge emerged in the county as just such a provincial centre, *Durolipons*. The site had always been strategically important: it was on dry land, with a convenient river crossing, easily accessible from the

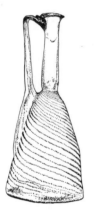

Glass flagon from Barnwell

Cam valley, the chalk belt and the great fenland river routes. The Celts had settled there, and upriver at rival Grantchester. It was the Roman decision to fortify Castle Hill and direct their roads on that fort which determined this rivalry. The hastily-constructed fort of A.D. 61 was replaced a decade later by a strong palisade following the alignment of Akeman Street. Around this developed a maze of timber buildings on Mount Pleasant, spilling down towards Madingley Road. Quantities of household goods have been found here. A ring of nearby settlements was established at Arbury, Barnwell, Newnham, and Grantchester. By A.D. 200 this was the most populous part of upland Cambridgshire and its acknowledged centre.

Roads and cities were—as the name implies—an intrinsic part of Roman 'civilisation'. What is special about Roman Cambridgeshire is its splendid system of fenland canals. This had a dual purpose—to increase trade, and aid drainage. The greatest was Car Dyke, now an unimpressive banked ditch best seen at Goose Hall, near Landbeach. The dyke falls into three sections, only one within the county: an artificial straight cut, five miles long, connecting the Cam at Water-beach to the Great Ouse. Further cuts in the Soke and Lincolnshire created a through route to Lincoln and York. Its commercial importance can be seen in the vast quantities of pottery dug up near Waterbeach at the harbour of Clayhithe. Not all came to *Durolipons*. The Romans also built four canals connecting villages on the chalk belt to the Cam—the lodes at Bottisham, Swaffham Bulbeck, Reach and Burwell. Reach Lode in particular was a thriving trade route, with Upware a major port. Clunch quarries at Reach provided the stone for many of the finest buildings in the county. Further north a remarkable series of channels was dug with an eye to drainage rather than trade. The 'Rodham Farm' canal, the straightening of the Great Ouse north of Littleport, diverted the drainage of the peat fens from Wisbech to King's Lynn. This avoided the 'dam' of silt deposited by the sea in the Wisbech outfall during the previous 200 years.

These canals, and a maze of lesser ditches since lost, opened the fenlands to settlement in the 2nd century A.D. The extent of occupation can be exaggerated. A Roman map of the fens north of Ely would have shown little but marsh and mere. The principal settlements occurred in the 'higher' areas. The southern fens between Cambridge and the Isle were assiduously ditched and planted. Other occupied areas were the silt fens, the lands beside the fen islands, and the 'roddons', sinuous silt strips in the peat fen deposited by extinct rivers. Roddon settlements reached deep into the southern fenlands. One example is Butcher's Hill, north-west of Littleport, beside the Old Croft River. Excavations have revealed ditches, irregular Celtic

Roman stylus

fields and 18 hut sites built on platforms against the shifting ground. Jugs, bottles, potsherds, bones, grindstones, and coins from A.D. 80 to A.D. 270 were also unearthed. Today, there are not 18 buildings within a mile radius of this settlement!

This degree of occupation implies some form of co-ordination. Much of the fenland was probably imperially owned, drained and farmed for state profit. Fen farmers would have been smallholders, on short-term leases, living in rectangular wattle-and-daub houses with clay floors. Produce varied though grain was farmed everywhere. In drier areas, like the fen edge between Cottenham and Fen Drayton, and the islands of March, Manea and Stonea, wheat was usually farmed —elsewhere it was spelt or barley. The fens were a granary for legions in northern Britain. Aerial photographs also show droves and pens for cattle, sheep and horses, and summer pastures on marginal lands. In the far north there were saltworks, including one major pan at Norwood Marsh. There were no cities or villas, and few villages—but the fens were more intensely farmed than for 1,000 years following.

The centre of this imperial venture was the old Icenian site at Stonea. There the Emperor Hadrian built c. A.D. 130 a complex unique in the Empire: a fort, palace and administrative block, with stable area, barracks, and slave quarters to serve them. The dimensions of the site are uncertain at the time of writing, since excavations continue. Its centrepiece was, however, a building of 80ft. by 30ft., and 60ft. high—towering above the imperial fenland estates. A mass of finds here have shown the lavish construction of the headquarters. The building was tiled, had four storeys, and walls 4ft. thick painted on the inside to resemble marble. It also had painted windows, an immense luxury outside Rome itself. The stone bath house adjoining included the usual mosaic floors, hypocaust and elaborate ventilation system. The size of the excavated area—currently about twenty acres—indicates the importance of the fens to the emperors, and of this site in particular. The Stonea Grange palace appears to have stood, however, for only about seventy years, until the beginning of the 3rd century A.D. Coin finds end in this period, with the reign of the Emperor Severus.

Life under the Eagles

The fens apart, Roman settlement clung to the valleys and chalklands in the traditional centres of occupation. The claylands remained predominantly forested, save for major penetration in the valley of the Bourne Brook at Comberton and Barton, with sporadic clearances elsewhere. One favoured area was the Granta valley, with settlements at Linton, Bartlow, and Horseheath. The most common settlement was the single farm or hamlet, but there were also several large villages and villa estates. Villas existed at Ickleton, Swaffham Prior, Bartlow, Comberton, Landwade, Girton, and Horningsea. The largest was on Ashwell Street, by Litlington. A rectangular building with courtyard, it had 30 rooms, including a bath house, hypocausts, mosaic pavements and painted wall-plaster. Its shortest side exceeded 100 yards in length, though this was exceptional. In most other cases, the impression is of comfort rather than wealth. The vast majority worked on the land, as peasants, slaves or smallholders. Farming mixed arable and pastoral, as in the fens—a combination of large granges and small, hedged, 'Celtic' fields.

What were these people like? Much can be learned from their goods. A wealth of material survives—much of it for the wealthy. Five bronze mirrors in the Museum of Archaeology and Ethnology indicate the importation of luxuries from the Mediterranean. The quantity and quality of metal goods far outstrips anything hitherto known. The commonest metals were still iron and bronze, used respectively for common and higher-quality domestic goods. Skillets, jugs, brooches, lockets, bracelets and bowls attest to the skill of Romano-British workers in bronze. Hoards have been found throughout the county, from Litlington, Willingham and Burwell to Flaggrass on the fen causeway. Iron was also used for all these goods, and for everyday objects such as keys, pins, chains and spoons. Many came from workshops in Great Chesterford, the ore being mined in the Nene valley at Old Sulehay. Other base metal is rare, but includes three splendid pewter jugs and a solid-looking lead table from Burwell. Pewter and lead were new materials in the metallurgical record of the area. So, too, was glass—and Cambridgeshire has produced some excellent flasks, miraculously preserved through 2,000 years. These were again luxury goods, ranking with semi-precious jewellery made of jet, amethyst and sardonyx—found in different parts of Cambridgeshire.

The commonest finds are pottery, from coarse native-fired pots up to fine imported Samian ware excavated from villas. Much native pottery came by canals from the Nene valley and barge loads were lifted from the riverbed at Clayhithe and Upware. Castor and Stanground were centres of production, their pots being typically colour-coated with a metallic glaze, some bearing hunting scenes. The main rival to Castor was the pottery from Horningsea. Conveniently situated above the Cam, the potters' works occupied an area of 14 acres, every yard yielding broken pottery. Seven kilns were found in one season's excavation, each fashioned as a basin in the ground with a lining of fired clay, and a stone 'tunnel' above leading to a flue. Pots were

Pottery kiln (of the Castor type)

27

wheel-thrown, then piled up from the bottom of the kilns under a dome of straw and clay plates, and fired with charcoal. The result is functional rather than beautiful: lead-grey pots coloured by the fumes, almost one inch thick, with deep rims and minimal decoration. These reflect Belgic influences, contrasting with the Continental appearance of those from Castor. Other potteries, at Jesus Lane in Cambridge, produced colour-slip imitations of Samian ware for the quality market. There is the same contrast between these goods and between the bronze or iron tools seen above and the bone or leather implements used by the poorer classes.

It was a highly stratified society. The slave was bound to serve his master; the peasant tied to his land. Social distinctions are never clearer than in the rituals surrounding the death ceremony. Poorer people were interred in mass cemeteries like those at Guilden Morden, Madingley Road, Cherry Hinton, and Hauxton Mill: more boneyards than cemeteries, where previous burials were ruthlessly disturbed to accommodate later bodies. Grave goods were unpretentious. Some cemeteries, such as Litlington, serving villas, were more orderly and well-appointed. Still further up the social scale were burials in stone *mausolea,* like one at Arbury Road, which was 14ft. by 16ft. in size, and contained lead-lined coffins, and grave goods including seven Samian vessels, five glass jugs, and an iron lamp to light the corpse's way to death. The most prestigious burials were in barrows—either interment in an old round barrow, or construction of a special mound. Barrow burial reached its peak in the amazing 'Hills' at Bartlow, close to a villa-place in the Granta valley (*see* Plate 2). Excavations in 1832 produced enormous quantities of grave goods, of all types and of uniformly high quality. All, tragically, were lost in a fire at Dunmow in 1847.

Burials tell us much also about religion. The number of children buried with coins on their eyes, to pay Charon's fee, confirms belief in the vitality of paganism in the first three centuries of Roman rule. A special place is reserved for a series of bronze statuettes from Willingham and fen-edge villages, including a naked figure of Mercury with his cloak and laurel wreath, and a head of the Emperor Commodus. The latter shows the strength of emperor-worship in the imperially-owned fenlands. Other favourite deities were Diana, Venus, and Hercules, whose local statues include elements associated with the Celtic god Taranis, allegedly worshipped at Wandlebury. Some consider that an existing temple at the Ring assimilated the two, continuing the worship. Increasingly, however, the county followed the Empire into Christianity. Cremation replaced inhumation as the favoured rite, in graves aligned on an east-west axis. Numerous

Willingham bronze bust of Emperor Antoninus Pius

Christian objects survive from the region: a baptismal bath from Burwell; and a pewter communion cup from Ely with the Alpha/Omega and Chi/Rho symbols. From across county boundaries come two magnificent hoards of ritual silver objects—the Mildenhall and Water Newton Treasures. The latter is particularly prized, as the earliest find of such goods from the Empire. Dating from the late 3rd century, the hoard comprised a shallow dish, two bowls, a goblet, a hanging bowl, a strainer, two superb flagons, and 17 votive plaques, all bearing Christian symbolism. Both hoards now rest in the British Museum.

Decline and Fall

These treasures were made in difficult times. Roman security was threatened in the 3rd century by a series of imperial pretenders. Raids by Saxon pirates made the seas hazardous. The reigns of Diocletian and Constantine saw British coastal defences reorganised under the Court of the Saxon Shore, and *Dux Britanniae,* but this only delayed attack. In A.D. 367 a three-pronged assault by Saxons, Picts and Scots breached Hadrian's Wall and the Saxon Shore alike, and raiders penetrated deep into the province. The disorder these incursions caused are evident in the region. Villas were abandoned. Cambridge was fortified by walls of Northamptonshire limestone, 8ft. thick, with a ditch 10ft. deep and over 30ft. across. Settlements across the Cam in the Round Church area were evacuated. Coin hoards reflect the insecurity of the inhabitants. The Nene valley factories ceased production and fen settlements declined as flooding wrecked the drainage system. The economic, as well as military and political superstructure of the region began to decay. The evacuation of Roman troops in A.D. 407 by the pretender, Constantine III, opened the province to further invasion. Three years later, Emperor Honorius formally abandoned Britain to its own devices.

III The Coming of the English

The Age of Settlement (A.D. 400-600)

The English settlement in East Anglia is a matter for controversy. Some scholars consider it a warlike invasion which expelled the Celtic population; others believe that a peaceful colonisation took place over generations.

The evidence is uncertain. The earliest English settlers were clearly warriors, yet apparently came in peace. There are numerous Anglo-Saxon graves in Celtic cemeteries, with signs of honour. The only large pagan cemeteries, beneath St John's College playing fields, co-existed with British settlements on Castle Hill, at Girton and Grantchester. These may, however, have been from garrisons of *foederati,* like similar sites at Lincoln and Norwich. Federates were important in the second phase of settlement. Their rebellion in Kent in A.D. 442 began a wave of invasion; the two generations following were decisive in the English takeover of East Anglia. By A.D. 500, Anglo-Saxon finds in Cambridgeshire greatly outnumber Celtic ones.

Typical Anglo-Saxon bronze fibula

The newcomers were Angles, a Germanic tribe from Jutland. Their graves suggest a strong, warlike people dominated by the fighting male. Warriors were buried in state, with shield, spear and shortsword (*seax*) beside them, and lavish bronze brooches and clasps. Women were buried with domestic goods—girdle-hangers, symbolising their control over the household, and stone and bone spindle-whorls. These finds are quite unlike Celtic goods in design, bearing new abstract, geometrical and animalistic motifs. Their pottery shows not only difference, but degeneration. Wheel-thrown British pottery gives way to crude, hand-coiled pots with thick walls and poor glaze, easily mistaken for Iron Age ware.

Their distribution reveals the spread of English settlement. The Angles were skilled in the use of shallow vessels, and the sluggish East Anglian rivers were their highways into the heart of Britain. The Nene, Ouse and Cam valleys were therefore the first part of the county occupied. By A.D. 500 colonisation had reached beyond Cambridgeshire, to Maxey, St Neots and Lakenheath. Cambridge was quickly occupied. Settlement spread up the Cam tributaries, with early villages at Linton and Haslingfield, and along the chalk belt from Newmarket to Balsham. The Angles took over British sites, giving them English names. Only a bare half-dozen Celtic place-names remain in the county, such as Girton, Comberton and Chatteris. Celtic idiom has similarly vanished from our dialect.

This was therefore an invasion, although one lasting many decades. What became of the British? Cambridgeshire provides no mountains for refuge and the clayland Celtic settlements had returned to forest by A.D. 550. Some were undoubtedly massacred—a mass burial by Heydon Ditch is one possible site. Many became slaves, others retreating south-west along the chalk belt. Yet in one part of Cambridgeshire, the fens, Celts may have survived. Neglect of the Roman engineering works and land subsidence after A.D. 450 reduced drained fenland to marsh, isolating Ely and other islands. Here lived a dark-haired, independent people, the Gyrwe, first recorded in the enigmatic 7th-century *Tribal Hidage*. Reference in local monastic and borough records to Welsh names and 'Welshmen' in later centuries suggest the Gyrwe were partly Celtic. In the words of the 6th-century monk Gildas, they alone 'persisted in their faith, in the lands of their fathers'.

Pagan belt-buckle from Wilbury Hill

Abbeys and Earthworks: the 7th Century

English control in upland Cambridgeshire was disputed between three tribes. The west (together with much of the East Midlands) belonged to Middle Anglia, the far south to the East Saxons, the rest to East Anglia. Warfare was incessant during the 7th century. The dominant power at first was East Anglia, and Redwald and his successors subdued Essex and forced Middle Anglia back along the chalk belt. These early military successes, however, proved counter-productive. Middle Anglia was swallowed by the powerful Middle kingdom, Mercia, under its great king Penda. Penda then attacked East Anglia, defeating her rulers, Sigebert and Anna, in A.D. 653–4.

Most scholars believe that it is due to this conflict that the four massive dykes were built at Heydon, Pampisford, Balsham, and Reach, identical in design and function. On the west side ran a deep ditch filled with brush. Rising from this was a steep, grassy slope to a rampart or *vallum* where defenders stood. The earthworks ran parallel to each other, crossing the chalk belt between natural defences of fen and forest. Heydon and Brent Ditches have been ploughed flat, but Flean Dyke and Devil's Dyke remain magnificent sights (*see* pl. 4). King Anna established his court by Devil's Dyke at Exning, for better defence. The dykes did not, however, deter the Mercians, and by A.D. 700 East Anglia had become a conquered province.

The most significant constructions in fenland were monastic. Early English looked on the fens with horror; the *Life of St Guthlac* calls them 'vast marshes, with here a black pool of water, now foul

A bronze workbox from Burwell cemetery

31

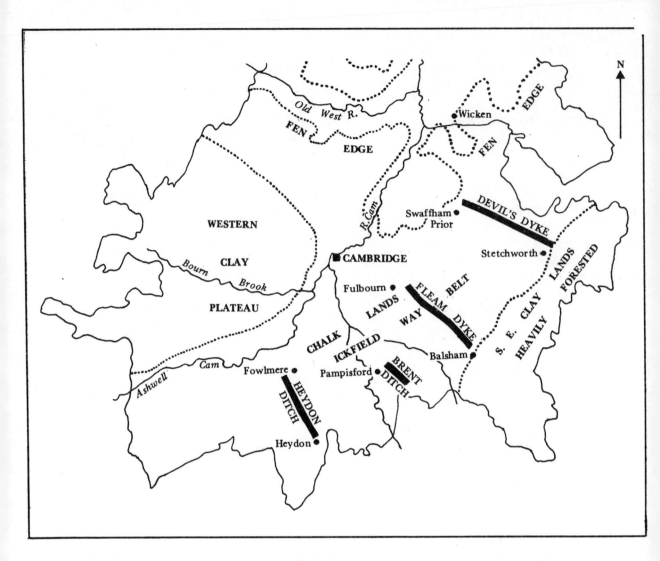

This map shows the position in Southern Cambridgeshire of the county's four largest ancient earthworks—the Dykes or Ditches at Stetchworth, Balsham, Pampisford and Heydon. Some scholars have thought these to be relics of the warfare between Iceni and Catuvellauni in the period before the Roman conquest (see Chap. I). The lack of Roman remains and comparison with other Anglo-Saxon earthworks (e.g. Offa's Dyke, on the Welsh border) make a 7th-century date more probable. The Dykes are aligned in parallel, the defensive ditch and bank facing invaders along the chalk belt from the south-west. Flooded meres and fens at Fowlmere and Fulbourn made Heydon Ditch and Fleam Dyke barriers connecting two naturally impassable areas, the southern end of each lying on forested clay. This alone would imply a military earthwork rather than the pastoral barrier controlling cattle and rustling postulated by some historians.

5. Anglo-Saxon strip lynchets in southern Cambridgeshire, by Heydon. The lynchets terraced hills for easier ploughing. These lie close to the defensive earthwork of Heydon Ditch (6th-7th century).

6. A typical fenland drove in the Isle of Ely before the 1939-45 war. Droves like this were concreted as farm roads after 1940 by WAEC (War Agricultural Executive Committee).

7. 'The Nearest Way Out is the Farthest Way Home'. This Victorian portrayal of the fens in the mid-18th century is less fanciful and more realistic than might appear!

8. A storm brews over the fens at Burwell. Note the twin chimneys of the sugar-beet processing plant, ahead.

running streams, also many islands, reeds, hillocks and thickets', the haunt of demons and disease. Two forces propelled the religious into this wilderness. One was their rejection of the world and expectation of an imminent second coming. The other was the favour of the Mercian and East Anglian royal houses, contending in shows of piety as in marks of war. By granting fenland estates, kings could display devotion at little cost, and extend control over wilder areas of their kingdoms.

The Cross of St Guthlac, near Crowland

Several abbeys were built on the fens at Crowland, Thorney, and Peterborough. The greatest was Ely, founded by East Anglia. Since Redwald (616), East Anglia had been noted for royal piety. Sigebert and Anna had been particularly devout. The former established England's first bishopric under Felix, and showed favour to the Celtic mystic Fursa, before personally retiring to a monastery. Anna's daughter, Etheldreda, influenced by Felix, pledged her virginity to Christ in childhood, keeping that vow despite two political marriages—first to Tonbert of the Gyrwe, bringing Ely as her inheritance, and then to the Northumbrian prince Ecgfrith. Faced with demands from the latter for consummation, Etheldreda fled to sanctuary in the Isle, establishing in 672 a double abbey of monks and nuns under her as abbess. The abbey prospered. Etheldreda in death left the abbey her vast fenland estates, which were further increased by the next two abbesses, also daughters of the royal house. Etheldreda's shrine became a centre of pilgrimage allegedly uncorrupted by decay. Rich offerings were made, including a magnificent ivory casket from Gundersheim and pendant of gold, crystal and precious stones.

Middle-Saxon Cambridgeshire (700–850)

The drama of the 7th century was followed by 150 years of peace, interrupted only briefly in the early 9th century when East Anglia followed Wessex in freeing herself from Mercia. Archaeological evidence shows gradual expansion and achievement. Finds include items of quality design and manufacture, such as a magnificent glass beaker excavated near Dry Drayton. The art of wheel-thrown pottery was re-introduced, highly-glazed Thetford and Stamford ware was found throughout the county as well as further down the Icknield Way. House sites improved. Early Saxon 'houses' were extraordinarily primitive, some no more than covered pits. Later sites in Cambridgeshire have produced post-holes from much larger, wooden buildings, 50ft. by 20ft., together with smaller thatched cottages of wattle and daub.

Green-glass pagan beaker, Dry Drayton

33

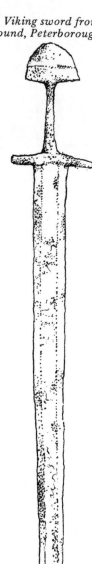

Viking sword from Stanground, Peterborough

This expansion came from an agricultural revolution. The distribution of cemeteries and finds by date indicate an enormous growth in the area of settlement. Large tracts of clay upland in the west were stripped of forest, and ploughed. Some silt fenlands in northern Cambridgeshire were re-colonised. Villages everywhere became larger, some hamlets coalescing to make a single settlement. Field patterns began to take the shape familiar from Domesday Book—two or three open fields, one lying fallow, the others divided into furlong strips of ridge-and-furrow, allotted among the peasantry. This piecemeal distribution may originally have come from systems of divided inheritance; but it was soon formalised, with apparently a deliberate realignment of fields throughout Cambridgeshire in the 9th century, to fit the needs of the strip system. As settlements grew, so did population and trade.

'The Fury of the Northmen' (850–1066)

The Viking invasion of East Anglia was sudden, and overwhelming. The invaders again came from Jutland, using the fenland rivers as their highroads into England. Written records like the *Anglo-Saxon Chronicle* leave no doubt of its violent nature. The first major incursion was in 866, led by three sons of the freebooter, Ragnar Lodbrok. Halfdan, Ingvar and Ubba defeated native forces and began an organised campaign of plunder. Their armies were reinforced each spring from Denmark and finally extinguished all East Anglian resistance at the great battle of Thetford (870). Five years later, a second wave arrived, under Guthrum and Oscytel. These established their standard in Cambridge, before striking south-west against Wessex. Alfred the Great's heroic defence needs no description here. It did little immediately to help East Anglia, and at the peace of Wedmore, Cambridgeshire became part of Danelaw.

The 150 years of peace in the middle Saxon period were now followed by 150 years of intermittent, bitter conflict. In 905, Edward the Elder of Wessex entered the county, overrunning 'all the lands between the Dykes and the Ouse, all as far north as the Fens'. Sixteen years later, the English finally reconquered East Anglia. A lifetime of peace followed, until the reign of Ethelred. The new millennium was ushered in to the sound of battle. Spirited defence at Maldon in 991 and a major victory in 1004 spared East Anglia from the worst of the Danish atrocities. This ended with new Danish invasions in 1010, and disaster at the battle of Ringmere, near Thetford:

> There were the Danes horsed; and afterwoods took possession of
> East Anglia, where they plundered and burned three months. They

moved deep into the wild fens, burning, slaying men and cattle; and Thetford they burned, and Cambridge.—Anglo Saxon Chronicle.

At Balsham, raiders tossed children in the air to be caught on spears. At Hadstock, a lone Viking was flayed alive after plundering the church; his skin remained nailed to the church door until Victorian times. The climax came in 1016, in six battles between the Danish king Canute and Ethelred's son, Edmund Ironside. The last was at 'Assandun', possibly Ashdon on the Cambridgeshire and Essex border. Canute's victory led eventually to undisputed control over England, and, in celebration, he built a minster church upon the battlefield. Hadstock church, with its fine Saxon fabric, may be this minster.

From this outline, one might expect the Danish impact on Cambridgeshire to be considerable, yet the archaeological record emphasises rather the continuity of English occupation. Only Toft and Bourne have Danish place-names, both being in forested claylands cleared during the 10th century. Scandinavian influence on arts and designs have been identified, notably in stone-carving, and some minor earthworks discovered. Otherwise, the development of the county towards Domesday society and economy continued apparently without interruption. This period actually saw the formal creation of the county, in two parts. The Isle of Ely became a legal unit in 974, as an area over which the abbot had exclusive jurisdiction. South Cambridgeshire emerged during the struggle against the Danes, the 'army of Cambridgeshire' swearing loyalty to Edward the Elder in 921 separately from other East Anglian forces. Cambridge, the county town, acquired in the 10th century its own defences (*burh*), courts, guild, market, and mint. Settlement broke from the Roman enclave on Castle Hill into the market area, with outlying villages at Barnwell and Girton. With a population of 1,600, it was one of East Anglia's largest cities.

Grave cover (from Cambridge Castle)

Continuity in trade and government was paralleled by the continuing importance of religious life. The 10th and 11th centuries saw progress in laying out parish boundaries, and building churches. Cambridgeshire is fortunate in remains, with much fine Saxon work at Hadstock and St Bene't's, Cambridge. Ely cathedral contains an outstanding example of late-Saxon sculpted stonework, Ovin's Cross.

The abbeys were, however, the religious heart of Cambridgeshire, before 1066. All were ransacked and closed by the Danes, but were re-established by Edgar (957–75) in greater number and estate. The new foundations included Ramsey and Chatteris; the former was granted huge estates in Huntingdonshire. Ely, re-established in 974, had an enviable ability to attract patronage. Byrhtnoth, *ealdorman* of East Anglia and hero of Maldon, presented nine Cambridgeshire

35

manors to the abbey after one lavish reception. An even more celebrated patron was Canute, who came regularly by boat to chapel services:

> Merry sang the monks in Ely
> As King Canute rowed thereby.
> 'Row, knights, nearer the land,
> And hear we these monks sing'.

Under the Anglo-Danish monarchy (1016–66), Ely rivalled Bury St Edmunds as the foremost abbey and shrine in East Anglia, if not England. Domesday Book records her wealth: 1½ hundreds of land at Mitford, Norfolk; 5½ hundreds about Wicklow, Suffolk; etc. Pilgrims flocked to Etheldreda's shrine. Edward the Confessor and other royal children were educated there. The abbots were great nobles, intimately connected with the fortunes of the monarchy.

The Norman Conquest (1066–70)

It is therefore appropriate that the last resistance to the Norman Conquest in England should have been at Ely. The Norman arrival in Cambridgeshire after Hastings was uncontested, but their heavy hand soon drove many into discontent. An underlying resentment of foreign invaders was one factor. Another was the imposition of a manorial economy. The worst affected were freeholding peasants (*sokemen*) of whom Cambridgeshire had many, and the thegns. The former were gradually made unfree, the latter suddenly dispossessed by Norman knights. It was with an English thegn that resistance began.

Hereward 'the Wake' is an enigmatic figure. He came from Bourne, in Lincolnshire, holding moderate estates as an armed man of the abbots of Croyland and Peterborough. The replacement of the English abbot of Peterborough by the Norman Turold in 1070 signalled Hereward's rebellion. Turold brought with him a reputation for severity —and 60 Norman knights to be settled on the thegns' lands. Hereward and other tenants fled to join Danish raiders occupying Ely. They were joined by men of power in the old Anglo-Danish monarchy: Earl Morcar; Bishop Æthelwine of Durham; and the land magnate Turkil Cild. An army accumulated; Hereward led daring river raids on Peterborough and Burwell. The rebellion was, however, doomed. King Sweyn of Denmark made peace with William in 1071, removing Danish support. William moved deliberately to crush resistance, supervising the siege personally from Cambridge. A blockade was established and flying columns of knights were despatched to deal with further raids. The main effort concentrated at Willingham, at the southern end of the Roman causeway to Aldreth. The causeway was painstakingly reconstructed, as a platform for invasion. One attempt failed when the causeway collapsed under the weight of armoured knights. Where assault failed, treachery succeeded. By threatening confiscation of monastic estates, William persuaded the abbot to admit the Norman army while the English were foraging for supplies. After a brief battle at *Aldreheda*, presumably Aldreth (the name is a corruption of Etheldreda), the Normans penetrated the Isle and took control. Cambridgeshire, and England, had entered the Middle Ages.

WILLIAM THE CONQUEROR.—From his Great Seal.

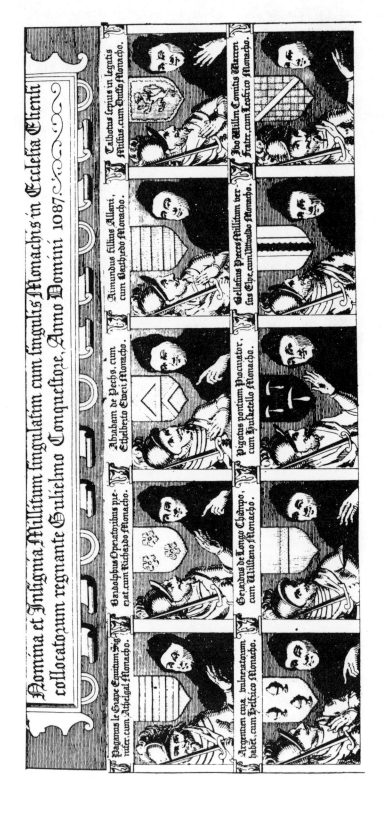

After the defeat of Hereward, Norman knights were stationed on the Isle and monastery. Knights and monks allegedly became firm friends—as this medieval illustration records.

IV Centuries of Growth (1066-1300)

The early Middle Ages were crucial in the development of Cambridge-shire. The cathedral came to Ely, the castle and fair to Cambridge. The forested wastes in the county were cleared and ploughed. Churches and other buildings survive in almost every parish, as evidence of expansion, supported by a mass of documentary evidence such as estate accounts, judicial records, maps, and Domesday Survey. It was that truism, an age of change.

Fortress in the Fens

Some things did not change. One was the political and ecclesiastical importance of Ely. While Cambridge was a market town serving the southern uplands, Ely was a bishopric, centre of a major group of church estates, and a political entity. It was also a refuge for people opposing the crown; Hereward's legacy dogged the Isle for more than two centuries.

The first occasion came in the disputed reign of Stephen (1135-54). Bishop Nigel was Henry I's treasurer, and staunchly supported his daughter Matilda's claims to the throne. Nigel secured Ely with a motte-and-bailey castle, accumulating supporters. In 1142, the Isle was seized by Geoffrey de Mandeville, Earl of Essex, who devastated the surrounding countryside, 'sparing in his cruelty neither age nor condition . . . Christ and his angels slept' (Peterborough *Anglo-Saxon Chronicle*). Stephen ordered the construction of castles between Ely and the uplands, at Rampton, Burwell, Swavesey, and possibly Cottenham. Giant's Hill at Rampton and Burwell Castle survive as rectangular, flat-topped mounts surrounded by dry moats and spoil heaps. None were finished. It was indeed at Burwell that Mandeville met his end in 1144, while attacking the half-built fort.

It was during this troublesome century that Norman castles at Wisbech, Knapwell, and Cambridge were refurbished, and a new fortress built at Castle Camps by the Earl of Oxford. A church and earthworks remain among fields to record their passing. Ely itself remained quiet until the reign of John, and civil war between barons and king. Rebels seized Ely in winter, preparing for a siege. Ironically, bad weather defeated them; the rivers around Ely froze, allowing royal troops to cross them, and the barons fled.

Their revenge came six months later, in curious fashion—

> John . . . [went to] Lynn, where he was received with joy by the
> the inhabitants, and received great presents from them. Then, journey-
> ing towards the north, in the river which is called Wellstream, by an
> unexpected accident he lost all his wagons, carts and sumpter horses
> with the treasures, precious vessels and all the other things which he
> loved so well; for the ground was opened up in the middle of the waves,
> and bottomless whirlpools swallowed them all up.

The jewels were not lost in the Wash. Roger of Wendover's account
shows that the accident occurred inland, on the river north of Wisbech.
A freak tidal bore, known locally as a shuff, cost John his valuables
and possibly his life, for he died a week later at Newark.

The fens again harboured baronial revolt in the reign of Henry III.
Supporters of Simon de Montfort gathered here under the banner of
'The Disinherited', repelling a blockade and raiding the uplands. This
disruption reduced the county's taxable value from over £200 to
nothing in 1267. This time, heat rather than cold proved decisive.
An exceptionally dry summer allowed the royal supporters to cross
the marshes and fight their way to Ely.

Cambridgeshire thereafter became a favourite royal visiting place.
Edward I and II stayed repeatedly at the bishop's palace, the Biggin
at Fen Ditton. Not all their interest was civil. Monarchs after 1300
chose bishops of Ely very carefully, from men bound closely to the
royal cause. Such precautions kept the Isle out of future mischief,
even in the Wars of the Roses. The castle remains, south of the
cathedral, to recall 'the fortress in the fens'.

Ministers and Monks

Despite this unrest, Ely thrived as an ecclesiastical centre. Before
1100, this was not the case; fines inflicted after Hereward's revolt
were followed in William Rufus's reign by nine years without an abbot,
when monastic revenues were milked by the king. It was Henry I's
accession and appointment of Richard de Clare as abbot which began
Ely's revival. In 1106, the minster church begun 20 years earlier was
completed. Three years later, Ely became a bishopric. The offices of
abbot and bishop were combined, as the cathedral itself was integrated
with the church and abbey. Both developed over a period of two
centuries, and though 12th-century disorders hindered early building,
the Prior's Door and superb South Transept survive from Henry II's
reign. Barnack Rag, Ketton stone from Northamptonshire, Purbeck
marble, clunch from Reach, and soft carstone from Ely itself were
used in later additions. Two of the cathedral's glories, the east end

presbytery and western galilee porch, were built by 13th-century bishops, Eustace and Hugh of Northwold. The last major wave of construction was in the 1320s. Ely was then in the hands of Bishop Hotham and two remarkable subordinates—Prior Crauden, and Sacrist Alan of Walsingham. They completed the Lady Chapel, with its fine carvings and unusual position off the north transept, in 1321. A year later, the central tower collapsed, destroying much surrounding masonry in the roof. Instead of rebuilding the tower, Alan of Walsingham constructed an octagonal lantern bridging the entire hole, with 32 separate windows. Weighing 400 tons, held aloft by eight oak pillars 63ft. high, the octagon bears a lifesize Christ in the roof, 162ft. above the ground, carved by John of Burwell. The lantern is unique in Europe. The Sacrist also built Prior Crauden's Chapel, and designed the chancel stalls with their entertaining misericords: a bear in a tree; Satan with two women; and Salome dancing. His death of plague in 1349 left a building which has not been substantially altered since.

Construction meant wealth. The see held estates throughout East Anglia, including 12 manors in Cambridgeshire and as many in Suffolk. The bishop maintained residences in the Isle (Ely, Downham), in upland Cambridgeshire (Balsham, Fen Ditton), in the fens (Doddington, Wisbech, Somersham) and elsewhere—notably Hatfield in Hertfordshire, and Ely Place in Holborn.

Her greatest rivals lay outside Cambridgeshire, at Ramsey, Crowland, Peterborough and Bury St Edmunds. Smaller houses inside the county at Thorney and Chatteris flourished. Piety and cash led to new foundations. Some were tiny, like the Hospitals of St John the Baptist and Mary Magdalene in Ely, or the Benedictine nunnery at Swaffham Bulbeck—an aristocratic house with six nuns and more servants. Among the largest was the Augustinian canonry at Barnwell, one of the richest in East Anglia. Land was granted in the west and south-east claylands to London's most popular nunnery, St Mary, Clerkenwell, by parents dedicating their daughters to a monastic life. There were Gilbertian canons at Cambridge, Fordham and Upwell; Hospitallers at Shingay, Chippenham and Wilbraham; and a nunnery at Isleham. The vitality of monastic life is illustrated by Denny Abbey. This first developed as a Benedictine cell of Ely, in 1159, but was transferred in 1170 to the Knights Templar as a hospital for their order. After the suppression of the Templars, the abbey eventually passed to an order of Franciscan Minoresses, whose house at Waterbeach faced flooding. The site today is an atmospheric collection of ruins, mounds and fishponds covering 15 acres off the A.10, and open to the public. Anglesey Abbey, at Lode, has more medieval stonework, but later rebuilding and landscaping as a country house have destroyed its spiritual air.

Sigil of St Mary's Guild, Cambridge

41

The lifestyle in these houses varied enormously. Most remained poor, some even took paying guests. Ely, by contrast, was more than comfortable. Its buildings included dormitories, infirmaries, a cemetery, a chapter house; a Painted Chamber, Queen's Hall, and other rooms for noble guests; a kitchen, buttery, refectory, and cloisters; and a Treasury for storage of wealth. Monks followed a daily routine starting with matins at 2 a.m. and ending at 6 p.m. with compline. Their duties included hospitality to the poor and travellers, education of nobles' sons, and estate management. Lay brothers did the manual work. The monks' varied diet included huge quantities of ale and wine from their own brewery and vineyard—some compensation for seclusion!

For sheer quantity of religious building, we must consider the parish churches. Cambridgeshire lacks many 'pure' Norman or early English churches, but has much early work incorporated into later buildings. The ground-plan of nearly all Cambridgeshire's churches is 12th century. Undoubtedly the finest period church is the Holy Sepulchre in Cambridge—a copy of its namesake in Jerusalem and one of only five round churches in England. It originally comprised a circular nave, vaulted aisle and small apsidal chancel. The arcade's eight thick pillars support a triforium, clerestory and vaulted roof. Much altered in the late Middle Ages, unusually sensitive Victorian restoration has enhanced its antique appearance, with 'Norman' zig-zag decoration on the west doorway. There is more excellent Norman fabric in St Bene't's, St Botolph's, at Hauxton, and Isleham. St Mary's, Bartlow, is rightly famous for its round tower and murals of St Christopher, St George and the Dragon, and St Michael weighing souls.

The most important fact about early churches is not, however, their quality or appearance, but their distribution throughout Cambridgeshire. This is considerable, and worth noting. It confirms that the period to 1300 was indeed one of growth.

The Round Church (St Sepulchre's), Cambridge

Fields in the Fens

This expansion was greatest in the north. The silt fens in Domesday Book were the least populated part of Cambridgeshire; just two families for every 1,000 acres, and under a single plough team. This compared with 20 families and four or five plough teams in the uplands, and six families and two teams in the southern fens. The only named village was Wisbech, small and poor. The 14th-century Lay Subsidy paints a very different picture. By 1330, the siltlands had passed south Cambridgeshire in population density and intensive farming. Siltland agriculture was predominantly pastoral, with some domestic cultivation of grain and pulses. Villages like Leverington and Tydd St Giles grew to serve the area. Peat fens, by contrast, remained outside the normal economic system of Cambridgeshire. Some settlement had occurred beside the fen edge and islands. The islands themselves had experienced the same population increase as the uplands. Such marginal reclamation left most black fens untouched.

The difference between silt and peat reflected not natural fertility, but drainage. The relative height of the siltlands after a series of marine floods opened that area to permanent cultivation. That same deposition caused fen rivers to 'back up', waterlogging the peatlands. Agriculture was precarious, requiring dry weather and tame seas. High tides in the late 13th century brought enormous devastation. Settlers threw up banks of earth against the danger, the greatest being the Leverington Sea Wall or 'Roman Bank', which was 15ft. in height, 6ft. wide at the crest, snaking around the Wash with breakwaters every furlong. Culverts through the bank allowed fen drainage at low tide. The wall was a formidable defence, against a formidable threat; a 15ft. tide would have flooded fens in Waterbeach, overwhelming islands like Thorney and Whittlesey.

The peat fens present a fascinating story, brilliantly told in Professor Darby's *The Medieval Fenland*. Some fens, on the isles and edges, were permanently cultivated; some was irredeemable marsh; and much was 'summer land', flooded during winter, but good grazing in drier months. Each had a distinct economy and lifestyle. The islands practised an agricultural similar to upland Cambridgeshire—mainly arable, in hedged fields, with cereals as the principal crop. Vineyards, orchards and market gardens existed, and even the occasional shrinking patch of woodland—'The woods have for the most part disappeared, and the fertility of the turf is such that the land converted to tillage bears corn plentifully; nor is it less profitable otherwise, being full of fair gardens, rich pastures, shady groves and lush meadows'. Other documents describe inroads into marginal lands like Deeping Fen— and of damage and frustration caused by flooding in these lowlands.

At the other extreme were marshlands, used for fishing, fowling, and the gathering of reeds and rushes. The number of fish caught, especially eels, staggers the imagination. Doddington, Littleport and Stuntney contributed 68,000 eels a year to the abbot-bishop. Eels became a substitute currency, measured in 'sticks' of twenty-four. *Liber Eliensis* talks also of 'waterwolves, pickerels, perch, roach, barbots and lampreys which we call water-snakes . . . sometimes the royal fish, the sturgeon, is taken'. Peasants owed labour services fishing, sometimes commuted to 'fish-silver' rent. In drier fens, the main

.IIII. TERRA EPI DE ROVECESTRE. *IN STAPLEHOV HVND*

EPS Rofenſis ten jn Giſlehā . I . hid 7 dim . 7 xx acs
ſub Archiepo Lanfranco . Tra . ē . III . car . In dnio . I . car .
7 xI . uilli cū . II . car . Ibi dim molend . II . sol 7 VIII . den .
7 ccc . anguill . Ptū . III . car . 7 II . mil anguill . Paſta ad
pecun uillæ . Val 7 ualuit XL . sol . T.R.E . LX . sol . De hac
tra tenuit Wluuin uenator regis . E . dim hid 7 xx . acs .
7 xII . sochi habuer . I . hid . sub Turbto qui oms 7 dare 7 uende potuer .

TERRA ABBATIE DE ELYG. *IN RADEFELLE HVND.*

M ABBAS De Ely ten *STVVICESWORDE* . Ibi ht VIII . hid
7 dim . 7 dim uirg . Tra . ē XII . car . In dnio . III . hid 7 dim .
7 ibi sunt . III . car . 7 duæ adhuc poss fieri . Ibi . xvI . uilli
7 v . bord cū . vI . car . 7 vIIma . poteſt fieri . Ibi . IIII . serui .
Silua ad . cc . LX . porc . Paſta ad pecun uillæ . Int
totū ual . x . lib . 7 tntd qdo recep . T.R.E . xII . lib .
H tra jacuit 7 jacet in dnio æcclæ de Ely .
In ead uilla ten Harduin de Eſcalers . I . uirg de abbe .
Tra . ē . II . bob . Valuit sep . v . sol . Hanc trā tenuit
Goduin . sz n poterat uende . Dim hid pti ht abb
de Ely in dnio in ipſa uilla . De hoc M ſupſit Seric
de Odburcuilla . I . uirg 7 dim de dnica firma abbis
de Ely . 7 poſuit in M S Wandregiſili . ut hund teſtat .

190 d

In *WESLAI* . ten abb . III . hid . Tra . ē . v . car . Ibi sunt . II .
7 adhuc . III . poss . ee . Ibi . IIII . uilli 7 v . bord . 7 II . serui .
Ptū . II . bob . Val 7 ualuit . x . sol . T.R.E . c . sol . H tra
jacet 7 jacuit sep in dnio æcclæ de Ely . teſtante hund .

M Ipſe abb ten *WARATINGE* . Ibi . IIII . hid 7 dim . Tra . ē
vII . car . In dnio . III . hid . 7 ibi . II . car . 7 adhuc . II . poss
fieri . Ibi . vI . uilli 7 III . bord cū . III . car . Ibi . III . serui .
7 ptū . I . car . Silua . xx . porc . Paſta ad pecun uillæ .

4 LAND OF THE BISHOP OF ROCHESTER

In STAPLOE Hundred

1 The Bishop of Rochester holds 1½ hides and 20 acres in ISLEHAM under Archbishop Lanfranc. Land for 3 ploughs. In lordship 1 plough;
11 villagers with 2 ploughs.
½ mill, at 2s 8d and 300 eels; meadow for 3 ploughs, and 2,000 eels; pasture for the village livestock.
The value is and was 40s; before 1066, 60s.
Of this land Wulfwin, King Edward's Huntsman, held ½ hide and 20 acres; 12 Freemen had 1 hide under Thorbert; they could all grant and sell.

LAND OF THE ABBOT OF ELY

In RADFIELD Hundred

1 M. The Abbot of Ely holds STETCHWORTH. He has 8½ hides and ½ virgate. Land for 12 ploughs. In lordship 3½ hides; 3 ploughs there; a further 2 possible.
16 villagers and 5 smallholders with 6 ploughs; a seventh possible.
4 slaves; woodland for 260 pigs; pasture for the village livestock.
In total, value £10; when acquired, as much; before 1066 £12
This land lay and lies in the lordship of the Church of Ely.

2 In the same village Hardwin of Scales holds 1 virgate from the Abbot. Land for 2 oxen.
The value always was 5s.
Godwin held this land, but he could not sell. The Abbot of Ely also has ½ hide of meadow in lordship in this village.
Saeric of Auberville took 1½ virgates of this manor away from the Abbot of Ely's lordship revenue and placed them in St. Wandrille's manor, as the Hundred testifies.

3 In WESTLEY (Waterless) the Abbot holds 3 hides. Land for 5 ploughs; 2 there; a further 3 possible. 190 d
4 villagers; 5 smallholders; 2 slaves.
Meadow for 2 oxen.
The value is and was 10s; before 1066, 100s.
This land lies and always lay in the lordship of the Church of Ely, as the Hundred testifies.

4 M. The Abbot holds (West) WRATTING himself. 4½ hides. Land for 7 ploughs. In lordship 3 hides; 2 ploughs there; a further 2 possible.
6 villagers and 3 smallholders with 3 ploughs.
3 slaves; meadow for 1 plough; woodland, 20 pigs; pasture for the village livestock.

A page from the Domesday Survey of Cambridgeshire showing the estates of the Abbot of Ely.

products were reeds, rushes, and sedge. This 'lesch' was cut for thatch, fuel and as building materials for wattle-and-daub huts. Here lived a mass of birdlife—geese, coots, dabs, duck, herons, etc.—captured in nets or trapped with birdlime. Hundreds were taken in each expedition.

The 'summer lands' combined two economies. During wet seasons they were hunting-grounds for fishermen and fowler. In summer they became grazing land of unparalleled fertility. Grass was sometimes left to grow until August, then cut for hay and put to pasture. More frequently, cattle would be transported in spring, often by boat, and left for summer grazing. Summer lands belonged to a fenland parish or parishes as common ground, according to complex rights and obligations. Parish and pasture might be miles apart; and parishes often argued about their claims to a particular common. Gradually lowered by turf-cutting, vulnerable to rain and sea, such pastures were a vital element in the fen economy.

Through the fens ran the rivers, the roads and drains of this area. Their upkeep was another duty of fenland tenants; records are full of disputes about services neglected, failure to dredge or cut a drain, to carry out boating duties or pay tolls. One parish's indolence was another's inundation. The fens demanded central management, by the landowning abbeys, and constant vigilance by their tenantry.

'High' and Dry—the Uplands

Growth occurred also in southern Cambridgeshire. The county Domesday Book is unusually detailed here. In 1086, most settlements still clung to the river valleys, chalk belt and fen edge. Inroads had been made into the western claylands, but the clay belt near Haverhill remained forested. Some of this woodland was 'useful'—as grazing for pigs, timber for fuel, fences, and houses, but most was untouched.

By 1300, the picture had changed dramatically. The south-eastern forest was reduced to isolated patches of open woodland, many showing in outline the mark of deforestation. Out Wood, below, is an example. Existing forest edge villages like Brinkley and Dullingham more than trebled in size, sprouting hamlet colonies within the new lands. Their '-ley' place-names themselves testify to forest clearances. Elsewhere, patches of waste and wood were similarly cleared for cultivation.

This expansion resulted from population pressure. Numbers doubled in Cambridgeshire between 1066 and 1300, as elsewhere. How far this indicated prosperity is uncertain. It undeniably brought wealth to the aristocracy. Cambridgeshire is rich in the trappings of medieval gentry. Churches contain oak and stone figures, brasses of knights and their ladies—such as this splendid example from Westley Waterless. There

Sir John Creke, 1324

45

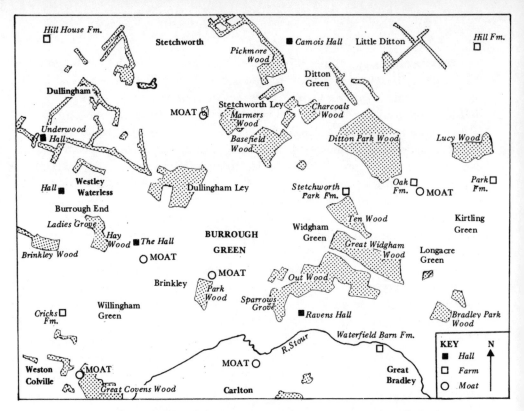

Moats, Halls and Woodlands in south-eastern Cambridgeshire.

are 300 moated sites, and numerous deer parks (Park Woods at Brinkley and Ditton are examples, with neighbouring moats). Parks were a source of meat, moats were useful as fishponds, flood protection and water supply. Both were also fashionable. Houses were similarly built with an eye to display. 'Chaundlers' in Linton is an example of an 'open hall', 46ft. long, 24ft. high, with a deep thatched roof. Originally, it contained only five rooms and the central hall reached to the eaves, without an upper floor, dormer window or chimney-stack. A fire was laid in the centre and smoke climbed into the rafters and escaped through a louvre. At one end was a parlour and chamber, at the other a kitchen and buttery.

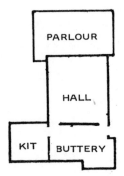

Plan of Chaundlers, Linton

Such apparently primitive conditions were infinitely superior to anything available to the peasantry. Rural life in this period is a matter of historical controversy. Traditionally, Cambridgeshire has been considered a typical manorial society. The peasantry lived in large 'nucleated' villages. Around each lay two or three open fields, divided into strips by corrugations of ridge and furrow, peasants holding a number of strips scattered throughout the area, and a cottage garden. Crops were rotated; one field for autumn wheat or rye; another for spring barley or oats; the third fallow for cattle. Disputes within the village might be settled communally, but all inhabitants owed allegiance

46

to the manorial lord; immediate source of justice, protection and taxation. To him were paid rents and fines, and services in kind or work on the lord's home-farm ('demesne'). Serfs with few or no strips provided paid labour for the lord, who owned the mill, and, indirectly, all land within the manor.

Like all neat pictures, this can be faulted in detail. Historical geographers have questioned the nucleated village and three-field system. Burwell grew together from five separate hamlets; Chippenham had 10 open fields. On the chalk belt and western fen edge, arable farming took second place to sheep farming. Research has shown some commutation of labour services into rent, and peasants abandoning their villages to take up lands elsewhere. This qualifies but does not disprove the traditional picture. It is unsurprising that, in an age of population pressure and clearances, new common fields were created and peasants forced to leave their bonds. Neither is, significantly, a sign of prosperity. Most peasants remained bound into the system, living in hovels of wattle, daub, and thatch.

Towns and Trade

Cambridgeshire is notable for the number of small market 'towns' that sprang up in the early Middle Ages. Some, like Linton and Kingston, were in populated river valleys on inland trade routes. More commonly, they were fen edge villages, connected directly to the fenland river trade. Swavesey, Soham, Reach, Burwell and Swaffham Bulbeck were examples, small ports importing trade goods and exporting local produce. Reach developed its own fair, supplied by barges and sailing ships down the lode from Upware. The clunch quarries and artificial hythe beyond Reach Green testify to the prosperity of this little town. For centuries therafter, such centres occupied a vital place in Cambridgeshire's commercial life.

The major towns of the region form three rings around and within the fenland trading system. To the north lay the outports, Wisbech and King's Lynn. Lynn became in this period the larger town, aided by the changing pattern of fenland traffic. Until the 13th century, Wisbech remained the outfall for the Cambridgeshire fens. Cam, Ouse, Little Ouse, and Wissey drained into the Wellstream, meandering north-west from Littleport down the natural line of drainage to Outwell, Elm, and Wisbech. The Nene joined this river in Laddus Fen, near Upwell. Lynn, by contrast, was served only by the Gay and Nar. Silting in the Wisbech estuary then forced the Wellstream to back up, spilling into a new channel, the Well Creek, which crossed the fenlands eastwards to Downham Market and then north to Lynn. The Nene

Carving from St John's Hospital, Duxford

47

later resumed a course to Wisbech, but the other rivers continued to Lynn despite vigorous efforts by Wisbech to dam the Well Creek at Outwell. Relations between the outports grew especially bitter, with multiple law suits and armed patrols.

The second ring of ports lay on the fen islands. Most, like Thorney and Ramsey, remained small, serving mainly their own inhabitants. Ely was an exception. A political and administrative centre, an abbey bishopric, an island large enough to produce its own trade goods, Ely was also connected by the uplands by three causeways—at Stuntney, Earith and Aldreth, the last on the high road to Cambridge. Brad Hythe at Ely contained a dozen warehouses, with workshops and factories. It was a planned development, built in the 13th century under episcopal orders. Ely had its own fair, on 17 October (St Audrey's or Etheldreda's Day) giving the word 'tawdry' to the English language! Never a borough, it was a commercial centre surpassed only by the cities at the fen edge.

These were Peterborough, Huntingdon, St Ives, and Cambridge. Each stood at the highest navigable point of a fen river, well served by roads. St Ives Fair itself possessed an international reputation, but paled by comparison with Stourbridge Fair in Cambridge— reputedly the largest in England. It was held in September, over several weeks, a shanty town of booths and tents visited by merchants of every European nationality. Spanish iron and Italian silks were exchanged for Baltic timber. Spices and jewels were bought, and fish sold.

In 1209 Cambridge became a royal borough, with a charter of incorporation from King John granting rights of self-government and justice by peers. Its price was 250 marks, and a military contribution of 20 soldiers in war time. A Merchants' Guild was established. The city is meticulously described in the 1279 Hundred Rolls. It had 17 parishes, 500 houses, and 75 shops. Only 70 houses remained in the old town, about the castle. The new centre lay about the market, south of the Cam. Between there and the river a maze of lanes led to the wharves, Flax Hythe, Salt Hythe, and Corn Hythe. These were served by two highways, High Street and Milne Street. Milne Street survives today only in Queen's Lane and Trinity Lane, terminating in college gateways. High Street remains under new names as Trinity Street, King's Parade, and Trumpington Street. With St Andrew's Street, it was the main highway out of the city. Cambridge's boundaries were defined by King's Ditch, a defensive earthwork strengthened during the troubles of Henry III with new bridges and gateways. The Ditch began at the weir by Laundress Green, struck east to Downing Street, crossed diagonally under Lion Yard to St Andrew's Street,

The first Common Seal of Cambridge

48

rejoining the river near Magdalene by way of Hobson Street and Park Street. A generation later, the Norman motte-and-bailey castle with wooden palisade was replaced by a stone fortress, with curtain walling, a barbican, two towers and an enormous gate-house. Within stood a great hall, domestic buildings and a prison. By 1300, the work was complete, dominating the city. To match this, Cambridge received by royal fiat the right to elect two burgesses, each serving in parliament as common members at the expense of a shilling a day.

But by 1300, Cambridge was already much more than just a commercial centre. The university had arrived.

Seal of Lawrence de St Nicholas, benefactor of Anglesey Abbey

V The Clerkes of Cantebrygge

The Coming of the Clerkes (1209–80)

The arrival of the university had an effect on Cambridgeshire as great in its way as any earlier invasion. From being an agricultural area with unusual commercial importance, the county acquired new international fame as a centre of learning.

The initial impact was, however, small enough, the 'clerkes' coming almost by stealth. Early medieval universities were not settled bodies of students and academics, divided by year and rank, inhabiting lecture rooms by day, and halls of residence by night, taking set examinations according to varied curricula. Basically, a 'university' was a gathering of respected scholars, sometimes living together for convenience, attended by students drawn by their reputation. Few students graduated. Many wandered between universities, seeking the best education or an escape from debts. Academics also roamed. 'Scholar' was often synonymous with 'traveller', 'traveller' with 'beggar'.

Cambridge developed by migration. The first was in 1209, from Oxford, after riots in that city. Further influxes from Paris in 1223 and Oxford again in 1240 made Cambridge a large, respected part of 13th-century scholarly life. This does not mean the teaching or institutions of the university would be recognisable today. Academics were indeed 'clerks', or churchmen; they taught a single curriculum of three subjects: grammar, rhetoric, and logic; designed to encourage clear writing, speech and thought respectively. (Their collective title, the *Trivium,* has added a disparaging word to the language!) Four lesser skills, the *Quadrivium,* were later added—arithmetic, geometry, astronomy and musical harmony. All were taught in Latin. Study concentrated on the few available works of classical scholarship, especially Aristotle. Books were few and expensive, and instruction came overwhelmingly through lectures. A degree of 'Bachelorship of Arts' took seven years to obtain; only then could students specialise in theology, law, or medicine. The drop-out rate was phenomenal, unsurprisingly. Students were usually boys, beginning university education aged 12 or thirteen. They were ill-disciplined, high-spirited, and sometimes violent. The first university powers granted by the crown were to discipline students, and proctors were introduced in 1261 after riots between northern and southern students. By 1270, town and gown assumed joint responsibility for public order. Cambridge life had already come under university influence. As early as 1235, tournaments and other raucous entertainments were banned from the area, lest they disturb studies. Local resentment to such interference was strong, with frequent attacks on 'clerkes'.

There was yet no geographical separation of town and gown. The universities possessed no buildings, and scholars and students lived and worked in rented rooms, usually in local inns. Certain places specialised in student accommodation, as 'hostels', varying from single houses with a few rented rooms to blocks containing 100 scholars. By 1280 there were 34 hostels, and several exclusively academic inns. Each hostel had its master; some had halls, chapels and gate-houses. There were not, however, colleges—yet.

The Coming of the Colleges (1282–1400)

The first college was Peterhouse, founded in 1280 under the will of Hugh de Balsham, Bishop of Ely. It housed a Master and six Fellows, with an endowed income linked to membership. Like most of its successors before the 16th century, it housed no students. They remained in hostels.

The next 70 years saw seven college foundations. In 1323, Chancellor of the Exchequer Hervey de Stanton founded Michaelhouse. It was followed 13 years later by King's Hall, founded by Edward II to house 32 scholars—the first college in either university to admit undergraduates. In 1338, a university house in Milne Street was converted into Clare Hall. In 1347 two new colleges, Pembroke and Gonville, were founded respectively by the Countess of Pembroke and the scholar, Edmund Gonville. They were followed within three years by Trinity Hall. Each developed its own strengths: Peterhouse for theology and medicine; Gonville for logic; and Trinity Hall for law. The last and richest of this first wave of endowments was by the townsfolk of Cambridge, through its wealthy gilds of Corpus Christi and the Blessed Virgin Mary. Corpus Old Court is the oldest surviving university building in Cambridge, and established a pattern for colleges closely resembling manor house designs. There was the same combination of Great Hall, gate-house and flanking wings, a quadrangular court about a lawn or yard. The hall contained the master's lodgings, a kitchen or buttery, and central area where scholars lived and ate. Wings were boundary walls or additional buildings—stables, guest rooms, or chapels. Gate-houses proclaimed themselves opulently, demonstrating the importance of the institution.

The original arms of Trinity Hall

Corpus was the last foundation for 70 years. Plague interrupted and almost destroyed the developing university, the rat-infested hostels

Butter measures used by the University to regulate trade

and streets being an ideal breeding place for disease. Cambridge lost a third of its population in 40 years, with outbreaks in 1349, 1361, and 1368.

Twelve years later came a different threat. The years before 1340 had seen increasing usurpation of power in Cambridge by proctors and chancellor. The chancellor could summon and imprison townsfolk for assaulting scholars. Mayors and bailiffs had to swear to maintain university privileges before taking office, and 'clerkes' were removed from the bishop's jurisdiction. Riots became common, including full-scale assaults on student hostels in 1322. During the Peasants' Revolt in 1381 Corpus Christi and Great St Mary's were sacked, the university chest was rifled and its records burned, the chancellor was forced to renunciate university privileges and take an oath to follow borough customs. A thousand men broke into Barnwell Priory, demolishing walls about former common lands. Only with the suppression of revolt did the university regain its dominance. Four years later, a fire swept through the city, destroying 100 houses. From the ashes rose a new Cambridge, with its own Guildhall by the market square. It remained a filthy maze of alleys, however, at least according to an Act of Parliament dated 1388!

The Second Wave (1440–1520)

The next wave of foundations began in 1428, when the Benedictines established Buckingham College at the bottom of Castle Hill. Many students were monks, and there was great competition in monasteries to secure university places and promotion. Abbots became concerned about the behaviour of monastic students. Living in communal hostels, mixing not only with secular priests but townsmen—and women— the monks found it hard to maintain their vows of poverty, let alone chastity. Buckingham College was the result—the first hall to house all its students on site.

Six colleges were established in the following century. In 1473, St Catharine's was founded by Robert Wodelark of King's—the final medieval foundation, but not the last to contain medieval stonework. That honour belongs to Jesus College, founded in 1496 by Bishop Alcock of Ely after suppressing the bankrupt nunnery of St Radegund. It incorporates many of the original monastic buildings. The refectory became the hall, the Prioress's rooms the Master's Lodge, and the church a chapel. Completion was delayed for 16 years by Alcock's death in 1500. By 1516, two more edifices were rising to grace the skyline, both owing their existence to John Fisher, one of England's leading churchmen, in scholarship and power. Master of Michaelhouse

52

in 1497, Chancellor after 1505. Fisher was also chaplain to the king's mother, Margaret Beaufort. She endowed first Christ's and then St John's, the latter standing on the old site of the Hospital of St John. A large brick court was constructed with a gate-house bearing the arms of England and France, the heraldic Beaufort antelopes, a Tudor rose under shield, and portcullises and crowns. Christ's, too, flaunts its dynastic frontage, emblazoning Tudor power and generosity.

This was not the first time a college was used for state propaganda. Undoubtedly the finest pre-Reformation colleges are Queens' and King's, both royal foundations of Henry VI and his wife, Margaret. Queens' was originally founded in 1446, as the College of St Bernard, but severe financial difficulties forced the President, Andrew Docket, to seek Margaret's patronage. The two courts at Queens' stand as monuments to the 15th century. The first court (chapel, library, kitchen and hall) was up by 1454, thanks to gifts and help by parishioners from Docket's church of St Botolph's. It was quickly followed by the gate-house (designed originally for King's), and riverside chambers connected by cloisters to make a second court. Edward IV's queen, Elizabeth Woodville, added her endowment a generation later.

King's rose much more slowly. Henry VI decided in 1441 to build a college, to match his endowment at Eton. Original, modest plans were abandoned for a grandiose scheme to accommodate a provost, 70 Fellows, 10 priests, 16 choristers and six clerks in a single, enormous court. The northern wing would contain the chapel, the east a three-storey building with central gate-house, the south and west a hall, library, lecture-room and chambers. Kitchens, a bakehouse, stables, and a brewery would occupy a side-court. Wide tracts of land in the commercial heart of Cambridge were compulsorily purchased. Five hostels, a church, a small teacher's college, Salt Hythe Quay and commons beyond the river were acquired, and the buildings demolished. Milne Street became a divided backroad. The first stone was laid in 1446, in the chapel—the only part of the plan ever completed. Some 'temporary' dwelling-places were erected, but no progress made outside the house of God. To this Henry granted a peal of five bells (the biggest in England, one weighing two tons), and special privileges including exemption from the jurisdiction of bishop, chancellor and even arch-bishop of Canterbury. It took eight decades to erect, interrupted by the Wars of the Roses, and was eventually completed by the Tudors. It stood 80ft. high, 40ft. across, and nearly 300ft. long, with the finest fan vaulting and stained glass.

First shield of King's College

Antagonism between town and gown meanwhile continued. In 1418 the Corporation petitioned the king, alleging interference, injustice and oppression. Chancellor John Rikinghale retaliated, demanding penance in the church of the Augustian Friars: 'Bilney offered to fight him; and when the Chancellor threatened to send him to the castle if he did not behave better to the university he replied that . . . he had a hundred fighting men to resist the Chancellor'.

Over 100 years later, another mayor was in the same place for the same purpose—on his knees, excommunicated, doing penance for ignoring university privileges!

'Little Germany'

Cambridge was the epicentre of the English Reformation. More than a decade before the royal divorce and papal crisis, reformation ideas were being discussed openly there. The brief stay at Queens' College of the great Dutch scholar and reformer, Erasmus, created a feverish intellectual climate in which Lutheranism took seed. Like-minded scholars met in the *White Horse* to discuss reform, giving the area the name of 'Little Germany', Hugh Latimer, later to achieve greatness and martyrdom in the service of Edward VI, announced his Lutheranism in 1525, from the pulpit of Great St Mary's. Latimer's colleague, Robert Barnes, was tried in Westminster the same year before Wolsey, for a similar sermon in St Edward's. Ely's diehard Bishop West sought to arrest the spread of such pernicious doctrines in the diocese by an oath condemning Lutheranism and other heresies. Cambridge-shire's proximity to the Suffolk seaports and reformist Holland made such precautions more necessary. Imported Tyndale bibles spread in the county, despite bans by West.

West died in 1533, replaced by the reformist Thomas Goodrich. Fisher was executed a year later, after refusing Henry VIII's Oath of Supremacy. The Reformation made Thomas Cromwell Vice-Chancellor, and the pace of change quickened. Monks and friars disappeared from the university, and Buckingham and other monastic 'colleges' were closed. A new college, Magdalene, rose upon Buckingham's foundation, established appropriately by Sir Thomas Audley, who became rich on monastic spoils through his office in the Court of Augmentations.

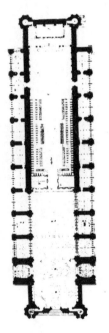

Plan of King's Chapel Confiscated monastic funds were used to endow five professorships, in Divinity, Law, Medicine, Hebrew, and Greek. Not all was gain. Libraries were ransacked and invaluable books burned for idolatry. Canon law was excised from the curriculum. The loss of the monasteries removed one avenue by which poor but able students could climb the academic tree. Cambridge became increasingly the place for rising gentry; as Latimer bemoaned, 'There be none now but great men's sons in Colleges and their father look not to have them preachers'.

Against this loss must be weighed one gem: Trinity College, founded in 1546 by Henry VIII as his memorial. It brought together several existing establishments—King's Hall, Michaelhouse, and a group of student hostels. Yet another wharfland street, Foul Lane, was grassed over to be part of Trinity, endowed with a Master, 60 Fellows and Scholars, and enormous revenues and privileges. The College took shape over the century. The chapel was not begun until 1555, and the Great Court dates from the late Elizabethan years of Thomas Nevile. He, too, built the second court, confirming Trinity as the rival of St John's in size and splendour. Only the gateway and buttery survive of earlier foundations, being from King's Hall and Michaelhouse respectively. As Henry's memorial, it is perfect, if only because much of its endowment came from monasteries he had dissolved!

Cambridge was active in the time of troubles after Henry's death. Arch-Protestant divines flourished under Edward VI, and Goodrich entered the royal council. Protestantism was promoted within the universities by Martin Bucer, Professor of Divinity, a controversialist of international reputation and proto-Calvinist beliefs. University churches led the way in adopting changes laid down by the state. Altars were replaced with common tables in the centre of the church, vestments were sold, and images defaced. Great St Mary's medieval frescoes were whitewashed over and replaced with sober scriptural texts. Cambridge theologians participated in drafting the two prayer books of 1549 and 1552. The university gradually translated its zeal to the city, Bucer preaching to large congregations of town and gown.

Great St Mary's Church

This makes Cambridge's part in subsequent events ironic. Edward VI's death in 1553 created a disputed succession between his next of kin, the Catholic Mary Tudor, and the Lady Jane Grey. The latter had the powerful support of Edward's leading councillor, Northumberland, her father-in-law. Mary fled to Norfolk, staying overnight at the house of Sir John Huddlestone, a staunch Catholic in Sawston. She left at the arrival of a Protestant mob to burn the place, promising Sir John a better house. The result is visible today as Sawston Hall. Northumberland pursued Mary with 8,000 foot soldiers and 200 cavalry. He stayed in Cambridge, and was received by the university—but his worsening political position, as the people rallied to Mary, made him acknowledge defeat while in the city. He proclaimed Mary himself, in Cambridge market-place, but still lost his head.

Mary's accession meant a purge of Protestants. The university's enthusiasm for reform made its plight the bloodier. The great Cambridge trio, Cranmer, Ridley and Latimer, perished in flames in Oxford. Goodrich was dispossessed, as were the Masters of every college but three. Fellows were expelled in number, St John's losing fourteen.

Only Catholics could take degrees. Village clergy were also purged. The only Cambridgshire martyr was John Hullier, formerly vicar of Babraham. On Maundy Thursday 1556, he, too, was burned, in the smoke of Protestant tracts: 'By chance a communion book fell between his hands, who received it joyfully, opened it and read so long till the force of the flame and smoke caused him that he could see no more ... His flesh being consumed, his bones stood upright even as if they had been alive, which the people afterwards took away, dividing them among them' (Foxe's *Book of Martyrs*). Catholic rule in Cambridge paradoxically brought at least one addition to that most Protestant university. In 1557, the Catholic scholar and royal physician, John Caius, became Master of Gonville College, spending his own money on a programme of expansion. Caius's long years abroad and admiration for classical styles are today visible throughout the College, notably in its three gates of Humility, Virtue and Honour. Gonville and Caius soon acquired a pioneering reputation in medicine, especially anatomy.

Autograph of John Caius

Elizabethan Cambridge (1558–1603)

The access of Protestant Elizabeth in 1558 meant another purge in Cambridge, and a return to former habits. The university remained close to royalty, and was visited by Elizabeth early in her reign. She arrived from Haslingfield on 5 August 1564, was escorted through the streets by the mayor and aldermen, then through the university by the Vice-Chancellor to a formal oration at King's Chapel. 'Mr William Masters of the King's Colledge, the Public Orator, making his three curtseys, kneeled down on the greese or step of the West Door, which was on the walls covered with verses, and made his oration ... when the public Orator began to praise the many and singular virtues set up and planted in Her Majesty. Her highness not acknowledging of, shaked her head, bit her lip and fingers and sometimes broke forth in these passions and these words 'non est veritas' and 'utinam'. But when he began to praise her virginity, she said to the Orator, "God's Blessing of thine heart; there continue".' This over, the Queen enjoyed her stay. She heard numerous services over three days, including music in the new descant style from King's choral school—lucky to have survived dissolution in the 1549 ban on chantries. Scholastic exhibitions, disputations and plays were staged, and enormous amounts of wine and beer consumed!

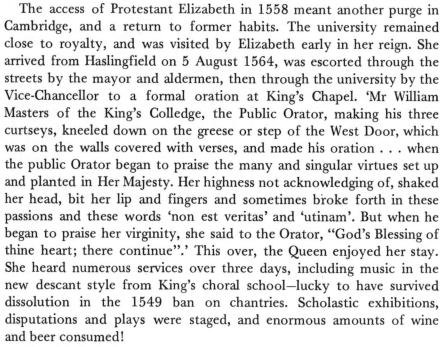

Interior view of King's College Chapel

What kind of city and university did Elizabeth see? Not much would have changed between her coming and the map, drawn by Richard Lyne in 1574. At the northern end were the remains of the medieval castle, now in ruins. Only the gate-house remained, in rather tatty

9. An interior view of the nave in the Round Church, Cambridge, showing the splendid Romanesque arches and corbelled heads of the 12th-century structure.

10. Denny Abbey contains monastic buildings from the 12th to 14th centuries, and incorporates (centre, right) an 18th-century house. Beside the abbey are fishponds, ditches and other earthwork remains.

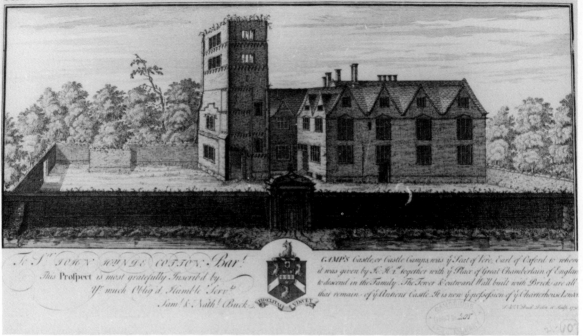

11.   An 18th-century artist's impression of the de Vere fortress and church at Castle Camps. Nothing remains of the early medieval castle except bumps and hollows. The church still stands, in open fields.

12.   The 17th-century church of Inigo Jones is all that remains at Thorney to mark its nine centuries as a monastic centre. The first foundation here was in 662 A.D.; the last was demolished in the Dissolution, to build Corpus Christi College chapel.

13. A Victorian artist's portrayal of the manor house at Anglesey Abbey clearly showing the house's monastic past. The Abbey is now open to the public.

14. The southern front of Childerley Hall, Cambridgeshire. Charles I stayed several days at Childerley after his abduction by forces of the New Model Army.

15. Sawston Hall, the 16th century home of the Catholic Huddlestons. An earlier house here was burned down in 1553 by Protestants seeking the fugitive Mary Tudor.

16. The magnificent south front of Wimpole Hall; the facade dates from 1742, but the house itself can be dated back in parts at best to 1640.

Richard Lyne's map of Cambridge (1574). The line of 'the Kinges diche' is clearly shown. (From the original in the Cambridgeshire Collection)

glory. The churches of St Peter and St Giles stand thereby. The map shows clearly the line of King's Ditch, and Barnwell Gate. The Ditch had become an evil-smelling dry sewer, and the marginal note in Latin suggests diverting the Vicar's Brook to clear it. This was done in 1610, by local worthies, including the famous Hobson of Hobson's Choice, who ran a coach service between his Cambridge and London inns. The resulting conduits, including the one that bears his name, removed Cambridge's last 'fortification'. Lyne's map contains detailed but inaccurate pictures of the colleges, and houses of religious orders long since dissolved. The general pattern of streets is familiar, but names have changed. Walles Lane is now King Street. One omission is the large number of inns we know of from other plans. One survivor today is the *Eagle* in Bene't Street, complete with original courtyard. The market is well displayed, with guild hall, prison, pillory and cross. Corn, butter and poultry were sold on its north side, vegetables in the centre, milk to the west, and meat in a shambles on the south, with a separate fish market in Peas Hill.

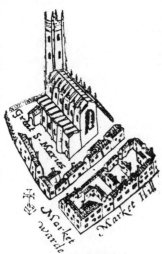

Central Cambridge in Tudor times (Hammond, 1592)

The university cannot just be mapped. It was an age of expansion. St John's built a second court, using a donation by the Countess of Shrewsbury. Two new colleges were founded: Emmanuel, founded by the statesman, Sir Walter Mildmay, as an expression of his own Puritan leanings; and Sidney Sussex, established on the site of a former Franciscan friary by Frances Sidney, Countess of Sussex. The Backs came for the first time into college hands after 1600, swampy commons becoming the magnificent lawns and avenues of today. Student members, too, expanded. By 1640, there were more students than for the following 150 years. Subjects of study remained the same. Theology remained of great importance—unsurprisingly, given the numbers of graduates seeking church livings. The Sunday University Sermon at Great St Mary's was an event, attended by most dons and students. Preachers were frequently figures of national importance, like the leading Puritan, Thomas Cartwright. The student body was widely divided by class. Increasingly, the gentry and professional classes decided on an extended education for their sons. Such students paid their own way, as 'Pensioners', many never bothering to take a degree. The remainder were divided into two kings: Scholars, who came to fill an endowed place, often linked to a particular school or area; and Sizars, comparatively poor students given board, lodging and education in return for servant duties. It was from this third category that many of the most eminent Stuart academics were to come.

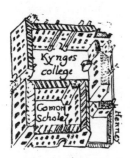

King's College and Common School (Hammond, 1592)

A student's life was in theory strictly regulated. The rules at Caius dictated a 6.00 a.m. start, and lights out at 8.00 p.m. Students were forbidden to gamble, visit taverns, go cock-fighting, bear- or bull-baiting, to have long hair or silken clóthes, or even see a play 'if it be in Englyshe'. Consorting with townsfolk was discouraged, and the Vice-Chancellor had special disciplinary powers to deal with adultery or fornication. The Protestant university seemed to be becoming a Puritan one. Violence, however, remained common. One affray in 1611 between students of Trinity and St John's led to whippings, deprivation of degrees, and even imprisonment for participants. It was a long way from the peace of Queen Elizabeth's visit, half a century before!

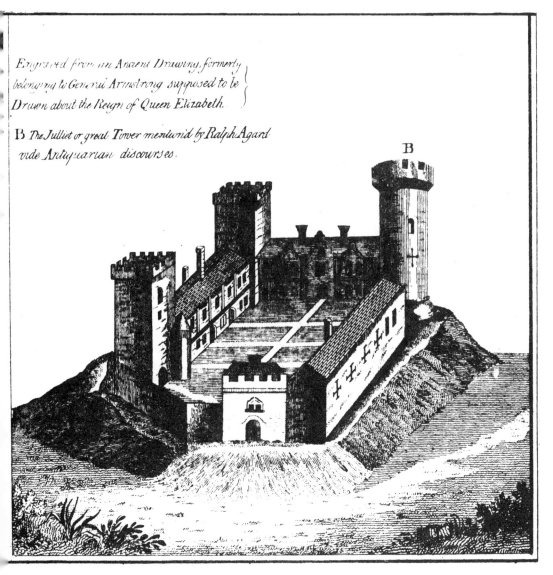

A rather fanciful illustration of Cambridge Castle drawn in Elizabethan times. By this date only the Norman mound and Gatehouse remained intact.

59

VI The Life of the County (1300–1600)

The three centuries after 1300 were transitional not only for the university, but the county. It was an age in which 'medieval' patterns of life and agriculture were broken, and replaced by new customs, in which the role of the church changed dramatically.

Stagnation and Disaster (1300–1380)

The 14th century saw an end to the continued growth on which previous prosperity had been based. The 1342 'Nonarum Inquisitiones' —a list of war taxes paid by each parish— show land abandoned throughout Cambridgeshire. The areas worst hit were the claylands, Horseheath, Weston Colville, Westley Waterless, Borough Green, and Dullingham in the south-east reported up to half their fields returned to waste. Croxton, Eltisley, Kingston, Madingley and Bourne in the west similarly recorded heavy losses, Guilden Morden suffering almost total extinction. Even the river valleys and chalklands on the fen edge fared badly. Bassingbourn lost 400 acres, and Impington 300 acres. The position in the fens is obscure; we are, however, told of flooding, 1,000 acres in Newton and Tydd St Giles was made unusable.

What caused this stagnation? Contemporary sources complain of low prices, heavy taxes, disease, a falling population: symptoms rather than causes of the malaise. One explanation is climatic. The early Middle Ages were warm and fruitful, with vineyards at Ely and other parts of Cambridgeshire. After 1300, records suggest a rise in sea levels coupled with longer winters and cooler summers. Newton was not the only parish beset by flooding and ice. A drop in mean temperature of one degree centigrade could knock a fortnight off the growing season. Marginal lands became uneconomic, population levels stabilised —and, then, abruptly, plummeted.

The Black Death cut a swathe through the towns and villages of Europe, moving, as a contemporary wrote, 'as fast as a man might walk'. In 1348 it reached England. For the next 20 years, bubonic plague ravaged the land. Its impact varied. At Dry Drayton, Cottenham and Oakington, the mortality rate was as high as 50 per cent. Three hundred and fifty of the diocese's 650 clergy perished. From Soham and Fen Ditton come records of tenements fallen vacant and labour services undone because there was no-one left to do the work. Shelford escaped

60

the first onslaught only to be decimated by new attacks in 1361. Elsworth and Bottisham, by contrast, suffered lightly. In all, perhaps a third of the population died from plague or famine. In prosperous times, such losses could be restored within a generation—but Cambridgeshire no longer had such resilience. By 1380, population had again stabilised—at a new, reduced level.

Cracks in the Mould (1380-1520)

Immediate effects were marked. There was a period of further economic slump in both agriculture and trade. St Ives Fair ceased operations for almost twenty years, and Stourbridge Fair did little better. The life of Cambridge and lesser market towns was brought to its knees.

The most enduring changes were, however, in the relationship between master and man—i.e., in the very nature of the manorial economy. The early Middle Ages were a time of scarce and expensive land, and plentiful and cheap labour. This kept the peasantry firmly bound to their manorial lords. In the 14th century this situation was abruptly reversed. There was now a glut of land, more than the reduced population could use. One consequence was a further reduction in cultivated land. Many woods and grasslands in Cambridgeshire bear the mark of ridge-and-furrow, where ploughed land was abandoned in the later 14th century. Another factor was the bargaining power of labour. Peasants leaving their lands illegally could find jobs, vacant tenancies, and complaisant landlords elsewhere. Landlords found it difficult to obtain the performance of labour services. The bondsmen gave way increasingly to the tenant, paying rent in cash or kind. Chippenham is one example. Its 15th-century record shows that customary services had almost entirely ceased, remaining peasants holding their lands by lease or rented copyhold. The low price of land encouraged the growth of a new, middling peasantry. While some peasants in Chippenham were labourers on the estates of the gentry, others prospered, acquiring lands of 30-40 acres—three times the customary size of a villein's holding. John Lenote had already accumulated 75 acres by the end of the century. Prosperous peasants sought to consolidate their strips within the open fields, producing solid blocks of land for more efficient farming. The yeomen emerged from the ruins of the manorial economy.

A primitive breast plough at work

These changes were not inevitable, and were resisted by landowners. There were repeated attempts to enforce the old pattern of subordination, by legislation and local agreements. These broke down. The most famous rupture was the 1381 Peasants' Revolt, partly a revolt against increases in taxation. Cambridgeshire lay on the periphery of rebellion, but had its share of violence. The assaults on the university and Barnwell Priory were matched outside Cambridge by assaults on tax collectors, sheriffs and J.P.s. Rebels seized and destroyed manorial rolls recording the labour services and dues of the peasantry. Shudy Camps rose *en masse,* leading an attack into the centre of Cambridgeshire. Robert of Leicester killed a J.P. at Ely, destroying documents. Neighbouring Littleport captured a tax collector and burned court rolls. Only swift action by regional authorities prevented a bush fire of discontent; Henry Despenser, Bishop of Norwich led an armed column through Cambridgeshire, hanging and burning. In 1382 there was more disorder, and proclamations were issued ordering the performance of labour services. But by 1420, the permanent commutation of labour services can be seen throughout the county—in Soham, Wilburton, and Chatteris, as well as Chippenham. The transformation from bondsman to tenant was almost complete.

A dibber (for sowing seeds)

Agricultural patterns also changed. With food prices low and labour costs high, landlords increasingly used cattle and sheep to fill their fields. Sheep were in particular demand, for England's expanding trade in woollen cloth. One centre of production was in Suffolk, and has left magnificent villages like Lavenham, Long Melford, and Clare. Cambridgeshire benefited to a degree. Traditional fenland pastures expanded rapidly. Upland villages saw the growth of sheep farming on an unprecedented scale. Some was undoubtedly the work of yeomen, on common land of small plots within newly-acquired holdings. Often, the impulse came from entrepreneurial landlords, supplying East Anglia's leading wool merchants. John Pygot and John Fisher were two such men, turning the parishes of Abington and Clopton into sheep-runs in the 15th century by enclosing the open fields with hedges. Enclosure was common throughout this period. An Inquisition of 1517 records enclosures at Cheveley, Childerley, Cottenham, East Hatley, Longstowe, Orwell, Shingay, and Steeple Morden, to which archaeologists would add Arrington and Tadlow. This, however, amounted to under 10 per cent of Cambridgeshire's cultivated acreage, much lower than in Midland counties.

It was a period of shrinking villages. The Plague destroyed no single settlement of size, although some hamlets like Whitwell and Clopton never truly recovered. Chippenham's population fell by half in the century after 1280. Houses fell into ruin. When pasture took over, still fewer cottages were needed; a survey of 1544 recorded whole streets as 'clere decaied', only six houses remaining in the entire village. This was a further 50 per cent reduction; yet tax records do not consider the village special, or worthy of relief. Field surveys at Great

Shelford, Boxworth, and Dullingham have produced evidence of abandoned cottages. Longstowe provides a splendid example of this decay, because it has never properly recovered. Today's village is a straggle of 20 houses along a mile of road, separated by plots of open, bumpy ground yielding pottery of the 15th century, but no later. This was a decay born not of depression, but a new form of prosperity with a smaller population.

The Life of the Church (1340-1520)

Cambridgeshire cannot boast the 'village cathedrals' of Norfolk and Suffolk, but it is not lacking in fine churches from the period. The church at Burwell undoubtedly comes closest to Perpendicular ideals; it has an enormous glasshouse, a stately nave, a fan-vaulted high roof alive with carved figures, a clerestory supported on slender pillars, rich panelling and canopied mosaics illuminated by a battery of windows. The nave at Leverington, tombs at Isleham, tower at Whittlesey, roofs at March and Willingham, and the porches and fonts throughout Cambridgeshire testify to the piety—and wealth—of their benefactors.

Traceried panel from Gamlingay Church loft

Contemporary ecclesiastical records, however, make unedifying reading. The main documents are judicial, and show a jaundiced picture of religious life. Barnwell Priory is a good example. In the early 14th century there were complaints by Cambridge men alleging enclosure of common lands, and extortionate rents and services. This was followed by an unsavoury succession dispute involving a native prior and a foreigner appointed by the papal Curia. The attack in 1381 followed generations of resentment between town and priory. Respect for the church reached a new ebb. This is the period of *The Canterbury Tales,* of lecherous priests and avaricious pardoners. Lollardy, an English heresy combining personal piety with distrust of clergy, became strong in East Anglia. Church officials visiting religious houses describe dereliction and sin. At Ely, the Sacrist had amounted £100 debts, and failed to repair the roof. The Prioress of Chatteris hoarded money meant to clothe her sisters, and consorted with one Edward Grange. Elm vicarage and churchyard were ruined through the vicar's negligence 'presentments of adultery etc. following'. Parishioners were frequently worse, but when Joan Herberd of Wisbech 'commonly defamed her neighbours, calling their wives "prest hore et monks hore"', her tale was likely enough to be believed!

A sober study of the diocese during the early 16th century indicates many faults. Many clergy were pluralists, absentee or both. John

Treguran, rector of Cottenham, held livings in Devon, London, Meeth, and Dublin, and was archdeacon of Kells. William Stockdale, vicar of Holy Trinity in Cambridge, appears in 1520 charged with poaching deer in the queen's parks, using his parochial assistants as gamebeaters. Clerical wills show a marked absence of books, especially bibles. Many priests were ordained despite ignorance of the Holy Scriptures or Latin. For a diocese containing one of Europe's foremost universities, it was disgraceful. So thought the reformers.

Dissolution and Reform (1520–1600)

The Dissolution of the Monasteries was in Cambridgeshire an event of enormous moment. The great houses (Ely, Ramsey, Thorney, Peterborough, Barnwell) and lesser establishments (Chatteris, Denny, Swaffham Bulbeck) profoundly influenced the religious and economic life of the county. Monasteries were lords to dozens of manors throughout Cambridgeshire, especially in fenland. They also exercised patronage over dozens of church benefices. All these passed into other hands: the bishops, colleges, and richer laity being principal beneficiaries.

The Dissolution itself was eagerly prosecuted by Bishop Goodrich, and carried out smoothly with monks and nuns compensated with annual pensions. Lay brothers who had done so much of the work maintaining monasteries were less fortunate. Few grieved the abbeys' passing, especially in areas where they had been hard landlords. Buildings like Thorney were systematically taken down. The lead from the roof was stripped and melted, and 140 tons of stonework was removed to build Corpus Christi chapel in Cambridge. Enough remained for the reconstruction of a parish church, in the 17th century.

Not only the monasteries suffered during this period. Chantries were abolished, and their clergy were 'released' for other work. Parish churches were inventoried, 'idolatrous' murals whitewashed, popish images, statues and vestments confiscated, and stone figures decapitated. The desecration of thousands of corbels by Goodrich in Ely cathedral remains today as a visible reminder of the age.

This orgy of destruction was followed by determined efforts to Protestantise the diocesan church. Goodrich consistently appointed dedicated reformists to church livings. The brief Marian interlude had little impact, because the new bishop, Thomas Thirlby, was too engrossed in government diplomacy to visit the see. Few Marian clergy resisted the Elizabethan Oath of Supremacy after 1558. The leading figure then was Bishop Richard Cox, who devoted himself energetically to reform. Cox now wanted a similarly comprehensive ministry. The

64

17. The Mill pool, Cambridge.

18. A panoramic view of Cambridge from the disused mound on Castle Hill, published in 1853. Note the undergraduate in gown and mortar-board.

19. Market Hill, Cambridge in the 1880s: note the parcels delivery van of the Great Eastern Railway (bottom left).

20. Ely Cathedral: the West door, tower and octagon. The amount of stone needed for the Cathedral is as staggering as its beauty. Most of the stone was transported to Ely by river.

21. Cromwell's House at Ely nestles close to the tower and West Front of the Cathedral. Cromwell lived here for 11 years (1636-47).

22. The Bishop's Palace at Ely, hard by the West Front of the Cathedral. The Palace was built by Bishop Alcock at the very end of the 15th century.

23. Looking out over the fens from the tower of Ely Cathedral.

troubles of the church after the Reformation had not produced the desired effect of an educated, preaching clergy. In 1560, Cox described only a third of his cures as well-served. Another third had absent vicars or rectors, and many were still held in plurality. One such pluralist was Thomas Goodman, who held churches in Great and Little Abington, belying his name: 'He servethe not ye cure of Lyttle Abington in due tyme as he oughte to do, and manye tymes uppon Satterdayes and hollye day evens he sayeth noe service at all, but ys aboute his owne busyness . . . more like a husbandman than a minister'. The poverty of diocesan livings (few were worth more than £20 per annum) made such behaviour inevitable. Preaching and churches suffered. At Waterbeach, 'the chancel is in great decaye, and yf it be not repayred in verie short time it will be utterlye spoyled and fall down'.

Cox launched a campaign to recruit literate clergy. This continued after his death in 1581, and proved successful. By 1600, almost every churchman in the diocese was resident, had been to university, and could preach. Fifty years earlier, only half the clergy could claim these distinctions.

This determined crusade under two bishops succeeded despite financial harassment. Henry VIII and his successors used their position over the church to drive unequal bargains with Ely. Goodrich was forced to exchange Hatfield House for a handful of manors in south Cambridgeshire, and to accommodate government ministers rent free in Ely Place. Elizabeth bullied Cox unmercifully, forcing him to yield half of Ely Place to a royal favourite and give up most of the diocese's estates in Norfolk and Suffolk. In return, Cox received some impropriate rectories and diocesan dues to the crown within the see. Ely was kept vacant for 19 years after Cox's death, while the revenue went to the crown. It was only filled after dean and chapter agreed to 'exchange' 34 manors for a further group of impropriate rectories, tithes and other spiritual portions—revenue belonging properly to the parochial clergy.

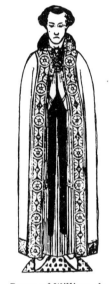

Brass of William de Fulbourn, 1391

The Protestant clergy inevitably influenced their congregations. Wills show progressively fewer references to the Virgin Mary and more to Christ alone as True Saviour. Some images were defaced by laymen, as early as 1540. The re-introduction of the Mass under Mary was resisted in several parishes, like Orwell. By 1600, many had gone further. Dissent was rare in Cambridgeshire, though Balsham and Ely briefly harboured two cells of the sectarian 'Family of Love'. The challenge generally came from within the Anglican church. The university fostered a growth in Puritan and Presbyterian sympathies, and a 'classis' was established at Dedham in 1582. Cox's own 'Low Church' sympathies meant the promotion of leading Puritans in

Cambridgeshire. Richard Greenham at Dry Drayton, Clement Martin at Tydd St Giles, and Richard Bowler at Leverington were particularly active, resisting Whitgift's campaign of conformity in the 1580s. Martin and Bowler converted the semi-Catholic northern fenlands to fierce Puritanism. The Jesuit William Weston described from his cell in Wisbech Castle the gathering of thousands of Puritans for meetings in town. Hours of sermons were followed by a cursory communion service, and a tribunal in which brethren confessed sins. It ended with extensive bible-reading, difficult passages being read and their meaning discussed. To Weston, it was 'a wretched and truly pitiful sight . . . comic and laughable' to see ordinary people in such debate. Goodrich, Cox—and Oliver Cromwell—would not have agreed.

A New Mould Forms

It is with the Tudors that we get the first imposing domestic architecture. If the castle and the church symbolise the Middle Ages, the corresponding image of the 16th century is undoubtedly the manor house.

There are in Cambridgeshire over a dozen fine manor houses dating from this period. Equally, there are records and memorials of the squires who built them. The finest buildings outside collegiate Cambridge were Anglesey Abbey, the two Halls at Madingley and Sawston, and Kirtling Towers. Childerley and Bourne Halls have claims to be included. Each belonged to a major family of country gentry. The Huddlestons of Sawston Hall have been touched on already. Justice Hinde of Madingley is an obscure figure. The most important builder was Lord North, of Kirtling. Chancellor to Henry VIII, his line remained close to the centre of power in later reigns. Elizabeth stayed here, passing through the splendid gate-house. Churches contain memorials to the gentry. The Cottons at Conington and Landwade, the Pepys at Impington are surpassed only by the polymath Sir Thomas Elyot, who lies in Carlton church. Scholar, author and diplomat, Elyot helped Henry VIII to divorce Katharine, was English ambassador to Emperor Charles V, and published many learned tomes. Lord North, too, can be seen in effigy, in a huge canopied tomb at Kirtling. Dozens of lesser memorials throughout Cambridgeshire record the resurgence of the Tudor landowning classes, often due to shrewd investment after the Dissolution. The prominence of the Wendys at Haslingfield reflected the acquisition of estates from Barnwell Priory; they did well from the residual Catholicism of others, as M.P.s, justices, and lawyers linked to the Protestant interest.

66

By contrast, the peasantry gained little from the Dissolution. They could not afford the freehold of their own land, and their new landlords were often more exploitative than the old.

It was a century of rising population, especially in villages of the chalk belt and fen edge. Willingham's population rose by 54 per cent in 40 years, and Cottenham's rose by 125 per cent. This strained limited natural resources, especially food and land. Wasteland was returned to the plough—but food prices still rose sharply, causing general inflation. This benefited landowners. Landless labourers paying high prices for food and competing for jobs suffered badly. Husbandmen—smallholders eking out a living with casual work—also suffered, becoming debtors during poor harvests and sinking into the labourer class. The yeomanry prospered, acquiring new acreage of 100 or 200 acres. Thus was created a middle class of farmers, and a lower class of wage-earning labourers, as today.

The change is brilliantly chronicled in Margaret Spufford's work on Chippenham, Orwell, and Willingham. As the title *Contrasting Communities* suggests, the picture was not uniform. Chippenham, on the chalk, experienced an enormous population increase, polarisation of the peasantry and destitution. The clayland at Orwell allowed less population growth, but enough for the same social effects. By contrast, Willingham was a fen village whose main resource was common land. A diversified economy including cattle, sheep, fish and fowl allowed even an expanded population to survive without alteration in the relative condition of inhabitants. Villagers here remained husbandmen, fiercely jealous of their right to common.

An ash and blackthorn flail

Common rights were enormously important in the Tudor period and enclosure was a popular scapegoat of the poor. Enclosure had, in fact, been more frequent in the previous century, but this did not prevent violent resistance against new incursions into common. The most explosive incident was at Landbeach, in 1549. Discontent was caused by Richard Kirkby's attempt to enclose two parts of common land after eviction of some copyhold tenants. Legal squabbles escalated into invasion of the fields by armed men, demolishing hedges. The authorities reacted swiftly. Landbeach was after all not far from Norfolk, where bad harvests and enclosures were creating peasant revolt under Ket. Even closer was an attack on estates near Cambridge, by men protesting against the same social ills. In the event, arbitration by the rector, later Archbishop of Canterbury, Matthew Parker, defused a confrontation.

Poverty, vagrancy and protest remained vital issues throughout the century. Bands of unemployed ('sturdy beggars') roused fears of disorder. The two solutions advanced were education and poor relief.

The former meant a rash of grammar and local village schools—Ely Diocesan Records reveal that there were 30 schools in Cambridgeshire in the 1580s. Peasants were desperate to achieve education at least for their eldest sons; 102 tenants at Willingham raised £100 a year to maintain the local school. In practice, schooling benefited only the yeoman classes. The necessity to have every pair of hands at work drove husbandmen and labourers to remove their children from school; those who did achieve literacy could use it only for perusal of bibles.

Poor 'relief' at first meant social control. Medieval control of poverty had been relatively efficient, organised through the church. Besides formal almshouses, donations of food, etc., there were religious 'Guilds' by which groups of people insured themselves against future poverty. These perished with the Dissolution, replaced by horrific laws on the treatment of vagrant beggars. One law even authorised enslaving vagrants (1547). This was widely ignored, but Cambridge and most parishes instituted patrols to catch beggars. These were whipped out of the area, to face the same harsh treatment in the next district. Only in their native parish could they obtain relief.

The replacement of this by mandatory Poor Rates was one of the greatest Elizabethan social achievements. In some areas, rates levied on residents to support the poor existed already despite government disapproval. One such was Wisbech, which had continued the work of its abolished Guild. Laws gradually applied this principle throughout England, and ordered the provision of materials for the genuine unemployed. Villages like Linton built 'Taske Houses' to house and employ the poor. The system was finalised in 1597, establishing parish rates. The workhouse remained, however, a place of last resort, usable only by a minority of paupers. Able-bodied and 'shiftless' beggars remained subject to the whip.

Being poor in Tudor Cambridgeshire was not as pleasant as the picture-postcard thatched cottages might imply. These were not the typical dwellings of the rural peasantry. A truer picture appears in the records of the Hearth Tax, describing one Cambridgeshire hovel: 'Not Chargeable. The House blown downe'.

VII Civil War Cambridgeshire

The Age of Laud (1603–40)

The arrival of the Stuarts made little difference to Cambridgeshire life. James I of England visited the county frequently, coursing hares around his hunting-lodge at Royston. The Earl of Somerset was arrested there, for murdering Sir Thomas Overbury. The Gunpowder Plot created some minor ripples, as a Catholic seminary (Nicholas Bastwicke) was imprisoned in Cambridge Castle for 'dangerous words'. A brief visit by James to the university in 1615 occasioned little more than a ban on smoking, and learned entertainments swilled down with wine. The principal Jacobean legacy was the fine wooden pulpits, panels and screens adorning many Cambridgeshire churches—including outstanding examples at Great Eversden and Great Shelford.

Charles I's reign was another matter. Charles was an Arminian, denying the Calvinistic doctrine of absolute predestination and determined to remove the 'excesses' of the Protestant Reformation. Conflict with the fiercely Puritan university, town and diocese was inevitable. The local campaign was waged by Charles's new Arminian Bishop of Ely, Wren. He directed parochial clergy to observe Archbishop Laud's new rubrics, including the placing of communion tables 'altar-wise' at the east end, kneeling communicants to receive the sacraments, wearing full ecclesiastical vestments, etc. Arminians were preferred to church livings and information about Puritan ministers supplied to Laud. Laud directed church life in Cambridgeshire directly, through long letters. The king used influence to elect his favourites as chancellors of the university—the Duke of Buckingham, then the Earl of Holland. Holland willingly enforced injunctions passed to him from the archbishop, many of which simply restated discipline. Students were forbidden to visit inns, bawdy-houses, or wear gaudy dress: 'Students do not wear clerical clothes, but new fashioned gowns of blue, green, red or mixed colours; they have fair roses upon their shoes, wear long frizzled hair upon the head, broad spread bands upon the shoulders and long Merchants' Ruffs about the neck, with fair feminine cuffs at ye wrist'. This 'High Church Puritanism' led to pointed criticism of college chapels and town churches. Trinity and Caius's services were 'scamped', given by laymen. Corpus Christi, Emmanuel and Sidney Sussex, known Puritan strongholds, used unconsecrated chapels. The practice of holding plays in Great St Mary's at

Hobson's Conduit (17th century)

69

commencement was attacked. A sermon there in 1632 by Mr Barnard of Emmanuel was treated as an attack on Laud and prosecuted before the Court of High Commission. Laud's interference was eased when he obtained rights of Visitation to the university, including commentary on all aspects of religious life there. Since academics were all clerics, purges become possible. An Arminian party grew up around Dr Cosens, master of Peterhouse, who erected a fine altar in the College chapel, and celebrated 'Roman' services.

Local resentment of these expedients was matched in the late 1630s by protests against the king's fiscal policies, and his refusal to call parliament. This occasionally became violent: 'A hundred or more of the inhabitants of Melbourne (whereof the collectors of Ship Money for that town were present) upon Friday the 12th of June instant did grevious wound and beat five or six of the Sheriff's Bayliffs and servants, they hardly escaping with their lives'. Collectors also met resistance at Babraham, and other villages. As the money was not forthcoming, and as rebellious Scots were being welcomed in the north of England, Charles reluctantly called a parliament.

The Age of Cromwell (1640-60)

Oliver Cromwell was very much a local man, from middling gentry. Educated at Sidney Sussex under Richard Howlett, he had sat in the 1628 Parliament as M.P. for Huntingdon, on the Grand Committee for Religion. In the next six years, he moved twice in the area. After involvement in disputes over the granting of a new charter to Huntingdon, he moved to St Ives, then took his uncle's previous post of tithe-farmer in Ely. Cromwell swiftly established himself politically, was active in local charities, and led resistance to the great drainage. His opposition to Bishop Wren was notorious, and he was a natural person for Cambridge to select as M.P. in the Short Parliament of 1640. His renewed position on the Committee for Religion then and in the ensuing Long Parliament included helping to dismantle the Laudian system. Laud was committed to the Tower in March 1641; Dr Cosens had already been dismissed, and Wren followed Laud into imprisonment within the year. College chapels were inspected and altars, crucifixes and other 'idolatrous' items removed. This followed petitions from Cambridge and the shire demanding a purge.

In the winter of 1641-2 the Civil War began to affect local Cambridgeshire life. In January, Charles left London. In February, parliament ordered the county to drill soldiers and purchase arms. Charles passed through Cambridgeshire in March, welcomed by royalists in the university, but ignored by the sheriff and county gentry. He raised his standard at Nottingham, and war began.

Cambridgeshire was strongly parliamentarian. An attempt was made at Ely by one of Wren's ministers to read the royal proclamation. Some fenmen joined Charles's army—enough for Ely and Wisbech to receive garrisons of parliamentary troops. More joined the parliamentary side. Cromwell was active in recruitment, commanding a troop of horse. After service at Edgehill, he helped to found the Eastern Association—a military league established in Cambridge in December 1642, between East Anglia, Hertfordshire and Huntingdonshire. The Association created a large, well-equipped army with high morale and religious zeal. Irs creation was timely. In February 1643, the royalist Lord Capel marched on Cambridgeshire, but was repelled. The Association was active throughout 1643-4, and its troops participated in the victory at Marston Moor (January 1644) that turned the tide to favour the parliamentary army. Ironically, Cambridgeshire, never a battleground itself, nearly became so in the last days, after Naseby. A fugitive with 5,000 men, Charles lunged towards Cambridge, capturing Huntingdon. A few months later, he was in the county again—in disguise, on his way to surrender to the Scots at Newark.

The end of the war did not end the county's significance in national and army politics. As negotiations between Charles and the two main factions in parliament, the Presbyterians and Independents, dragged on, the army became increasingly restive. In March 1647, Fairfax established the army headquarters at Saffron Walden, disobeying parliamentary injunctions to disband without pay. The army itself camped on Thriplow Heath. Eventually, army leaders decided on a bold move. Cornet Joyce with a troop of horse captured Charles from Holmby House in Northamptonshire, bringing him to the generals in Cambridgeshire. He spent several days at Childerley, the guest of Sir John Cutts, progressing finally to Newmarket by way of Chippenham Hall. The initiative proved ineffective. It tooks months of fruitless argument, a civil war between England and Scotland, and a series of local royalist risings (including ones at Ely and Linton) before a solution was reached—by removing the king's head.

The Impact of the War

The isolation of Cambridgeshire from the arenas of war did not protect it from the impact. Several parts of the county were fortified, the most notable remains being the Bulwarks at Earith, at the southern end of the Bedford Rivers. Cambridge was heavily garrisoned early

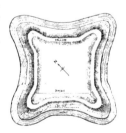

Earith Bulwark and Moat

71

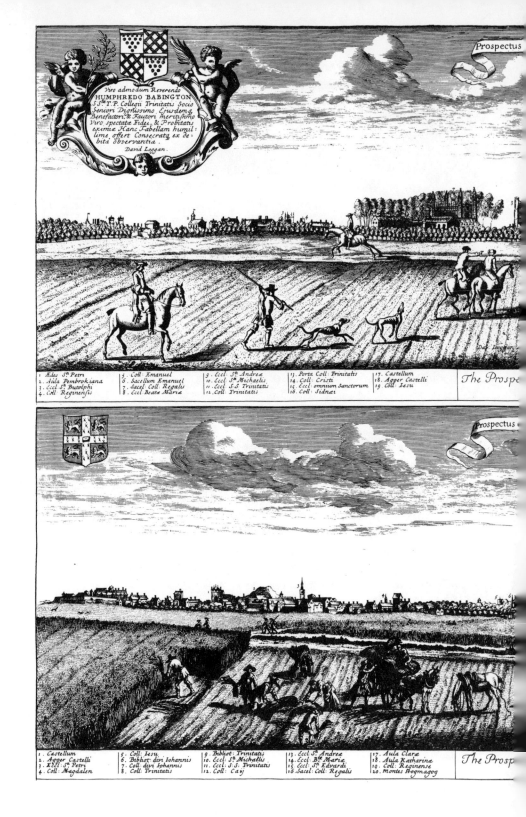

Prospects of Cambridge and its common fields from the east and west, in 1690.
(From David Loggan's *Cantabrigia Illustrata*)

BRIDGE *from*

1. Peter hous	5. Emanuel Colledge	9. St. Andrews Church	13. Trinity Coll. Gate	17. Castle Prison
2. Pembrok Hall	6. Emanuel Chappel	10. St. Michaels Church	14. ChrIst Colledge	18. Castle Hill
3. Butolph Church	7. Kings Coll. Chappel	11. Trinity Church	15. All St. Church	19. Jesus Colledge
4. Queens Colledge	8. St. Marys Church	12. Trinity Colledge	16. Sidney Colledge	20.

BRIDGE *from*

1. Castele Prison	5. Jesus Colledge	9. Trinity Libary	13. St. Andrews Church	17. Clare Hall
2. Castle Hill	6. St. Iohns Libary	10. St. Michaels church	14. St. Marys Church	18. Catharine Hall
3. St. Peters Church	7. St. Iohns Colledge	11. Trinity Church	15. St. Edwards Church	19. Queens Colledge
4. Magdalen Colledge	8. Trinity Colledge	12. Keys Colledge	16. Kings Coll. Chappel	20. Hogmagog hills

in the war, and earthworks built. The castle was occupied by Cromwell in August 1642, bridges were demolished, and defensive banks raised about the town. Only in 1646 was this system demolished, and the garrison removed. The city was administered during this period by military government, with soldiers billeted on the townsfolk and officers on the colleges. Armed men were drilled in college courts, and even in King's chapel. Permission was needed to leave or enter Cambridge and trade was strictly regulated.

The university suffered most, at least partly through the effects of war: 'Our Schools daily grow desolate, mourning the Absence of their Professors and their wonted Auditories . . . frightened by the Neighbour Noise of War, our Students either quit their Gowns, or abandon their Studies'.

The presence of royalist Fellows, especially in four colleges—Peterhouse, Jesus, St John's, and Queens'—did not help. In 1642, Charles appealed to both universities for donations, in cash or plate. Cambridge's contribution was small, and most of it was captured in an ambush by Cromwell; this did not, however, prevent, in 1643, a purge. The Vice-Chancellor was imprisoned for secretly printing royal proclamations. Fellows were later required to take an oath supporting the Solemn League and Covenant. Many refused, and were dismissed—like Peter Gunning, a brilliant ecclesiastical lawyer who delivered a blistering sermon against the Covenant in February 1644, before slipping across to the king at Oxford. Two months later, 63 Fellows were ejected. By contrast, the university as an institution survived unscathed. It was exempted from military service and taxed lightly. Its ejections were only part of a general parliamentary purge of clergy. The diocese's numerous Arminian ministers were similarly removed by a Commission under the Duke of Manchester. One such was the Reverend Mapletoft, of Downham: 'He usually preaches against the Parliament and calls them a company of wicked rebels, and ignorant people that are gathered together, and rob us of our goods, and calls us malignants, which would live without government, and cry down the Bishops'. The last reference is the more pertinent because of the local Puritans' sack of Bishop Wren's palace at Downham. Mapletoft refused to serve the sacrament except at altar rails, discouraged extempore prayer, and called Puritan preachers 'pedlars'. He was expelled on 6 April 1644. Manchester also appointed a Suffolk Puritan, William Dowsing, to clear the parish churches of all idolatrous images, pictures and objects. Thousands of such 'Popish marks' vanished. At Great Shelford, 112 superstitious pictures, three crucifixes, 12 cherubims and two superstitious inscriptions perished! Colleges escaped lightly, only Clare, Magdalene and Peterhouse losing portions of stained glass. It was this kind of Puritanism which led to a spate of witch-burnings, including no fewer than 13 in an assize at Ely during September 1647.

Churchmen and witches apart, the main losers were Cambridgeshire's few royalists, subjected to sequestrations and fines. John Russell, brother of the Earl of Bedford, paid £2,500 for his loyalties. Others did well from parliamentary service. Cromwell became Lord Protector to the Republic. His arch-spy, John Thurloe, built a mansion at Wisbech upon the previous castle site. Most neither gained nor lost. All had to pay the Cess, or army tax. This reached £3,000 a month for Cambridgeshire in early 1644, and remained at £550 a month even 13 years later. In the convoluted politics of the Interregnum, that was the county's main contribution.

A 17th-century fenland token from Wisbech

Restoration Cambridgeshire

The Restoration of Charles II in 1660 was celebrated in Cambridge, as elsewhere, with pomp and music, though joy was mixed with apprehension in this parliamentarian stronghold. In practice, few Cambridgeshire gentlemen suffered confiscation or fines. One predictable exception was Henry Cromwell, the Protector's youngest son, banished to his farm at Spinney Abbey, Wicken. One day, he had a strange visitor: King Charles, fresh from the Newmarket races, with all his court. Charles found the man farming contentedly, but naturally alarmed by the sudden attention. One lord seized a pitchfork and carried it before the farmer, explaining that he had been mace-bearer to Henry Cromwell in his days as Lord Lieutenant of Ireland!

Inevitably, Restoration was followed by purges in church, town and gown. Cambridge Corporation was suspended in May 1662, and 22 Puritan members expelled, including the mayor, Thomas French. College Fellows had to abjure the Covenant, or face dismissal. Royalist dons returned, including Peter Gunning, now raised to the Chair of Divinity at royal command. The return is neatly symbolised by the building of Trinity Library and Pembroke Chapel to designs by a nephew of the restored Bishop of Ely—no less than Christopher Wren. Wren's reintroduction of the classical style over a century after John Caius produced two architectural gems.

The biggest purge was in the church. Puritan ministers were expelled, Bishop Wren and his successors firmly suppressing all signs of nonconformity. Three casualties were the ministers Francis Holcroft, Joseph Oddy, and Henry Osland, now lying together in a little shrine in Oakington churchyard. The years after 1640 had inspired large numbers of local people with sectarian zeal. As early as 1660, a congregation of 72 Quakers were arrested at their Jesus Lane Meeting House. The Conventicle Acts of 1664 extended persecution to other sects. Dozens of warrants were issued by one Cambridge J.P. alone, for surprising and arresting conventicles. The principal sufferers were Cambridgeshire's large Baptist, Presbyterian and Congregational communities. Scores of dissenters were rounded up, fined, even imprisoned for their beliefs. High Anglicanism had returned—with a vengeance!

Oliver Cromwell.

VIII The Draining of the Fens

The Tudor Fenlands

The greatest alteration to Cambridgeshire was the drainage of the fens. Drainage was no new thing. The Romans had cleared large areas in the southern fenlands, though their systems were neglected and water returned during the Dark Ages. Piecemeal reclamation on the fen edge continued throughout the Middle Ages. One ambitious scheme was undertaken by Henry VII's minister, Bishop Morton, to protect estates near Peterborough. He cut a straight channel, Morton's Leam, 12 miles long from Stanground to Guyhirn, avoiding a long bend in the Nene. The Dissolution of the Monasteries however made concerted drainage impossible, by scattering abbey estates among 100 landowners. Control was left to Tudor laws and the Commission of Sewers. Both lacked power and were ignored. Commissioners were local landowners themselves, unwilling to offend neighbours by insisting on the maintenance of existing drains. The Commission had no power to cut new channels. Tudor fenlands were reached by floods, and high tides broke the Roman Bank in 1570 between Wisbech and Walsoken, flooding inland as far as Bedfordshire. This catastrophe prompted numerous schemes. One engineer proposed to drain the fens in six months, for only £5,000, and using 500 men. A patent was granted to Thomas Lovell to devise new drainage 'engines', and a Bill was passed in 1600 'for the Recovering of many hundred thousand acres of marshes'. All that actually occurred was some marginal reclamation, notably in Ely, Elm, and Soham. The Tudors passed leaving the fens in rather worse condition than before.

James I had little more success, despite local knowledge and high intentions. He declared that the 'honour of his kingdom' demanded drainage, and his Attorney-General advised new cuts to divert waters into the Lynn Outfall. Bills for general drainage were introduced, and failed. Lord Chief Justice Popham drained a large area around Upwell by a seven-mile channel connecting the Nene and Great Ouse. 'Popham's Eau' still exists, recalling his memory. A scheme launched by the Earl of Arundel failed. James decided to undertake the task himself, in return for 120,000 acres of reclaimed fen. This, too, failed, for lack of funds. Deterioration of existing drains created new flooding, notably in 1607 and 1613 (when Wisbech became an island). William Camden's *Britannia* (1607) pithily described fenmen:

a kind of people according to the nature of the place where they dwell rude, uncivill and envious to all others whom they call Upland-men; who stalking on high upon stilts, apply their minds to grassing, fishing and fowling. The whole Region itselfe, which in winter season and sometimes most part of the yeere is overflowed by the spreading waters of the river Ouse, Grant, Nene, Welland, Glene and Witham, having not loades and sewers large enough to voide away.

The Adventurers

Fen overshoes

After such talk and inaction, the decision in 1630 to undertake comprehensive drainage came as a shock. What was new was the calibre of the men involved. The men advancing or 'adventuring' the money included most major fen owners, led by Francis Russell, 4th Earl of Bedford. The family had received 20,000 acres of fenland after the dissolution of Thorney, and was promised 95,000 acres more if the scheme succeeded. His technical adviser was Sir Cornelius Vermuyden, who had been involved in reclamation since 1610, associated with James's schemes in 1621, and successful in similar projects on Hatfield Chase and the Isle of Axholme. His plan followed traditional principles—to straighten bends in the upland rivers, and thereby increase their speed of flow through the fens. Royal agreement was obtained, and the Adventurers acquired corporate status. Many opposed the schemes. Some despised Vermuyden as a Dutchman and Calvinist. Some, including Vermuyden's countryman and rival, Wester-dyke, believed the methods were fallacious. Instead he believed circuitous rivers followed the natural line of drainage, and that existing channels should be scoured, under tougher laws. Inland ports argued fervently on these lines, fearing the effect on river traffic of the new cuts. Others desired drainage but demanded exemption from the charges laid upon local inhabitants.

Many opposed all drainage because the traditional fenland pursuits of fishing, fowling, and reed- and turf-cutting seemed threatened. Pasturers objected to the loss of fertile summer grounds, and peasants saw it as an encroachment upon rights of common:

> Come, brethren of the water, let us all assemble,
> To treat upon this matter, which makes us quake and tremble:
> For we shall rue, if it be true, the Fens be undertaken;
> For where we feed off fen and reed, they'll feed both beef and bacon.

Navvies worked in the fens from 1631 to 1637, and their work was vandalised and destroyed by groups known as 'Fen Tigers'. Privy Council records show the destruction of ditches at Whelpmore, and confrontation at Wicken:

78

The people came out with pitchforks and poles, and gathered round a place where great heaps of stones were laid. Amongst them, John Moreclark, a principal rioter, was charged to obey the Council's warrant. When the messengers approached him, he pushed at them with his pike. The people prepared to assist him, and the women got together to the heap of stones to throw at the messengers, who were scoffed at and abused by the whole multitude.

Opposition notwithstanding, channels were cut: from Feltwell to the Great Ouse; from Whittlesey Mere to Guyhirn; from Crowland to Clow's Cross; and from New South Eau to Tydd. Morton's Leam was scoured, and sluices were erected at Tydd, Well Creek, Earith, and Wisbech. The old Bedford River was dug out from Earith to Denver, cutting nine miles off the Ely Ouse. In 1637, the 'Bedford Levels' were declared drained—prematurely. Flooding in 1638 led to a reversal of this decision and bankruptcy for many Adventurers. Bedford had to sell estates in Devon to meet his debts. Vermuyden was more fortunate as Charles I decided to complete the project personally, and appointed the Dutchman as technical adviser. The royal plans were visionary, including the construction of a royal palace at Manea linked to the Ouse by canal.

These high dreams collapsed amid civil war, which saw neglect and new flooding in the fens. In 1649, another Bill sponsored by another Bedford became law. Vermuyden was contracted to complete his work, and digging began anew. The North and Middle Levels were declared drained in 1651, providing the Corporation with land and revenues needed for the South Level. Work here included not merely scouring existing channels, but another enormous cut—the New Bedford, following its namesake. The area between them, the Washes, became an emergency catchment for times of flood. Other new drains included Downham Eau, near Denver, Tong's Drain at Nordelph, and the Forty Foot Drain. The work was dogged by sabotage; Cromwell on one occasion sent a troop of horse to restore order. In 1653, Scots and Dutch war prisoners were worked as slaves to complete the drainage. Ten years later, Bedford got his 95,000 acres; and in 1664 Soham Mere, the second largest fen lake, lay under grass.

It all seemed too good to be true.

Years of Frustration

The Level is intirely drowned; and there is not any Outfall, whereby to drain it: the Rivers, into which the Waters should discharge themselves, lie higher than the Lands: the Rain waters often drown the same Level.

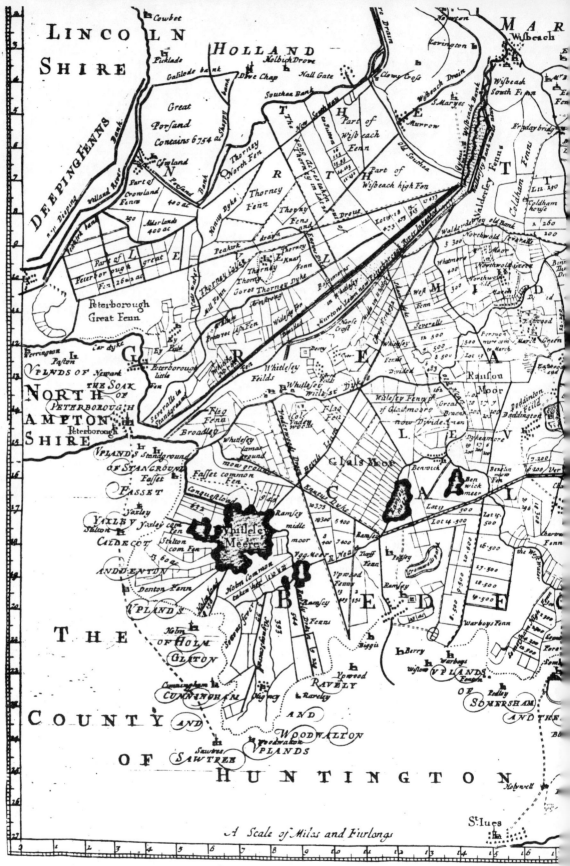

Sir Jonas Moor's map of the Great Levell of the Fens, 1684 (from a 1720 reprint in the Cambridgeshire Collection). Note the return of Soham mere and the continuation of inter-commoning fens, e.g. at Westmoor.

A MAP
of the
GREAT LEVELL
of the
FENNS
Extending into ye Countyes
of Norfolk, Suffolke,
Northampton, Lincoln
Cambridge, Huntington
and the Isle of Ely
Surveyed by
Sr Jonas Moor

I. Harris Sculp.

The speaker was a witness at a 1726 enquiry, into Haddenham Level. The fens deteriorated rapidly after 1700; no area was free from the threat of flooding and much lay permanently under water. As early as 1695, Celia Fiennes in her horseback tour of England was forced to ride between Ely and Sutton along raised river banks because the fens around were flooded.

An 18th-century coaster serving Wisbech and Lynn

No-one knew the solution. There were ideas in plenty in a host of contradictory pamphlets. Some blamed the Corporation, for failure to keep the drains scoured; others blamed 'selfish' farmers who by draining their own land too well had loaded water on to their neighbours. There were arguments about outfalls, and disputes between farming and trading interests. The Nene outfall below Wisbech was badly silted, and even the smallest ships had to unload in the estuary into boats. Some traced accumulations of silt as far inland as Ely and Earith, considering swift inward and slow outward tides the main problem. Merchants heaped venom upon the Denver Sluice, which had been built by Vermuyden to accommodate six rivers—the Bedfords, the Great and Little Ouses, the Lark and Wissey, and which was closed during high tide against incoming waters, and opened at ebb to allow waters downriver. During heavy rains the water downriver remained too high for the sluice to be opened, causing floods in the South Level. Opponents of the sluice prevented its reconstruction for 35 years, after wreckage during a storm in 1713. The fens, however, continued to deteriorate and disastrous flooding in the 1740s compelled reconstruction.

Debates were long and acrimonious; effects were mistaken for causes, and no one identified more than part of the problem. One cause went almost unmentioned. Peat is composed of spongy, vegetable fibre. Before drainage, it was 95 per cent. water in volume. Drainage had therefore caused an immediate lowering in land levels, as expected. Dry peat, however, continues to lose part of its volume yearly, through bacterial action. Turf-cutting, paring and burning of reeds also wasted the soil. From being 5ft. higher than the silt fens, the peatlands shrank to below their level—in some places, to below sea level. Water cannot flow uphill, and rivers flooded. Embanking rivers to run above the level of the peat in earthen 'aqueducts' created new problems. Peat banks collapsed, and had to be replaced with clay from pits at Ely and Upware. A more permanent problem was faced by the farmers whose lands were on the peat, and where drainage, ultimately, was through the rivers. The river banks were walls *against* local drainage! The solutions to these difficulties did not rely on a clear analysis of those agreed by all. Trial and error—and new technology—won the day.

82

Windmills and Watercourses

Good drainage required three things: a 'high-level' drainage system of rivers, outfalls and sluices; 'low-level' drains on the peatlands; and means of raising water between the two.

High-level drainage was the responsibility of the Corporation and its three constituent Boards. In each Level, there was activity. The South Level Board concentrated on maintenance and scouring. The Middle Level suffered from flooding of the Bedfords and Nene, and the silting of Tong's Drain. Regular dredging proved the answer. The North Level fared worse, as the Nene continued to back up above Wisbech and flood the fens. In 1720, Charles Kinderley proposed a new channel below Wisbech, but opposition by local merchants delayed the scheme half a century, until massive deterioration in the 1760s forced action, Once cut, the channel proved hugely successful, lowering waters in North Level by 6ft. Vessels of 200 tons could again reach Wisbech to unload.

Initially there was no system at all to promote low-level drainage. Ditches cut by individual farmers did often worsen drainage for neighbours. Drains cut by several farmers in different directions meant mutual misery. One result was the development of Drainage Commissions, established by Acts of Parliament to drain areas of fenland and charge inhabitants for the service. Commissions took over all local drains, linking them to a 'Main' or 'Engine' drain leading to the nearest river.

Between ditches and rivers lay a vertical chasm. It was bridged by the windmill. The windmill was imported from Holland in the 17th century, but did not become common until the 18th century after experiments with horse-drawn pumps failed. Very quickly, farmers turned to the windmill on a grand scale. Mills were uniform in design, consisting of four of five sails; a simple system of spindles and cogs; and a waterwheel with scoop blades at an angle to the water. In 1748, Thomas Neale counted over 250 windmills in Middle Level alone.

A fen windmill

But windmills could only be a temporary solution. The maximum height through which they could lift water was three feet, and as the peat shrank, this became insufficient. One solution was to build windmills above windmills, ascending the river banks in steps. Even this did not solve the inherent unreliability of windmills, and rain without wind reduced many fields to marsh. To observers in 1800, after years of flooding, prospects were poor: 'Two or three more floods will do the business, and 300,000 acres of the richest land in Great Britain will revert to their ancient occupiers, the frogs, coots and wild ducks' (Arthur Young).

83

A case in point is Burnt Fen, Prickwillow. The local Commission, established in 1759, built eight windmills in 15 years, assuming others from private landowners. From the start, activities were hampered by lack of money, contrary landlords, and shrinkage of the peat. By 1792 the first 'double-lifters' were planned, and introduced at great cost over 14 years. The Commission went bankrupt in 1807, and a new Act passed increasing their powers to raise revenue. Relief eventually came to hand. The sign of the New Lark engine said it all:

> In fitness for the Urgent Hour,
> Unlimited, untiring Power,
> Precision, Promptitude, Command,
> The Infant's Will, the Giant's Hand,
> Steam, Mighty Steam ascends the Throne,
> And reigns Lord Paramount alone.

Steam, Mighty Steam

The introduction of steam pumps did not on its own drain the fens. The early 19th century saw renewed efforts to improve the 'high-level' drainage system. The South Level Board was particularly active: introducing new sluices at Denver, Salter's Lode, the Hermitage, Earith, and Welmore Lake; embanking rivers; straightening the Ouse south of Littleport Bridge; and constructing the Eau Brink Cut between King's Lynn and Wiggenhall St Germans. Progress in the Middle Level was again hampered by long disputes over the Wisbech outfall. This continued deteriorating despite Kinderley's Cut, until sea vessels were unloading amid the sandbanks of Sutton Wash. Many favoured diverting the Nene to Lynn, by a 30-mile cut. The engineer Rennis advised two new channels around Wisbech itself, to improve the flow. Wisbech merchants as usual opposed both. The Nene diversion was abandoned for a shorter, Middle Level Drain, connecting Upwell to King's Lynn. The other scheme was forced upon Wisbech . . . and proved highly beneficial. A total of 3,000 acres of marsh were reclaimed, the river bed lowered 10ft. by natural scour, and navigation improved. Trade at Wisbech rose from 55,000 to 167,000 tons, in 20 years. In the North Level, it was Wisbech which led the fight for change, involving the destruction of dams above the town designed to irrigate the Bedford estates!

> These fens have oft times been by Water drowned.
> Science a Remedy in Water found.
> The power of Steam she said shall be employ'd
> And the Destroyer by Itself destroyed.

The first steam engines were installed after 1817, at Sutton St Edmunds and Upware. By 1850 there were 60 operating in the

Cambridgeshire fens alone and new designs were being introduced. Appold centrifugal pumps were demonstrated at the Great Exhibition, and immediately used to drain the last great fen lake, Whittlesey Mere. Crowds gathered to watch the drainage, many bearing baskets to carry fish. These were collected in tons and sold as far away as Birmingham and Manchester. At the bottom was a legendary pike and a hoard of medieval silverware lost *en route* for Ramsey Abbey. By 1853, 'the wind, which in the autumn of 1851 was curling the blue water of the lake . . . was blowing in the same place over fields of yellow corn'.

Since 1860, man's domination of the fenlands has been intermittently interrupted but never permanently challenged. Steam pumps were replaced in turn by diesel engines, before the First World War, and later by electric pumps. Each had advantages over steam in terms of fuel economy and easy running. Creation of the Great Ouse and other Catchment Boards in 1930 provided powerful impetus for new drainage cuts. The greatest changes came after terrible floods in 1947, when heavy winter rain and freak tides flooded 37,000 acres in the South Level alone. A Flood Protection Scheme designed by Cambridge University was instituted, which included a new sluice at Denver; a relief channel from Denver to King's Lynn; and the construction of the Cut-Off Channel. The last follows the fen edge, diverting upland rivers (Lark, Little Ouse, and Wissey) direct to Denver in times of flood. Coincidentally—or in accordance with the inexorable laws of fen drainage—it follows closely the line of a cut proposed by Vermuyden!

The Fen Economy

The history of the feudal economy after Vermuyden's drainage is inevitably one of change from a mixed, mainly pastoral economy to one based entirely on arable farming.

In the early period, pasturing of sheep and cattle remained the rule. Cattle in particular thrived, for example in the Washes. This was, however, complemented by a range of traditional fen 'industries'— fishing, fowling, turf- and sedge-cutting being the main examples. The fen rivers and meres remained a haven for perch, tench, bream, and pike. Eeling and fowling were other professional activities. Eels were captured in long wicker traps, or stabbed with glaives. Duck decoys were introduced from the Netherlands and used with nets. One favourite weapon was the punt gun, almost a small cannon. Day describes one 150lb. in weight, 10ft. long, and with a 2in. bore. The gun was fastened to the front of the punt and paddled towards the flock by a fowler lying flat in the bottom of the boat.

An eel-spear or glaive

85

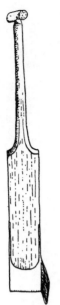

A becket

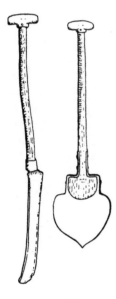

A turf-cutting knife and spade

Turf-cutting remained an important part of the fen economy into the later 19th century. Turfs were cut in spring, after surface water had been drained by March winds. Three tools were used: a knife; a sharp shovel shaped like the ace of spades to expose the peat; and a becket. The latter resembled a thin cricket bat with an iron flange at right angles to the tip. This would cut under and down one side of the turf, lifting it off with a twist of the wrist. Cut peat was dried in the summer and sold for fuel. Reeds and sedge were cropped for thatch. Reeds grew in the wetter fens, taking four years to reach the correct size. They were cropped in winter, after frost had stripped them back to the stalk, using a scythe or reed hook. Sedge was an autumn crop, used for cattle bedding as well as for thatch. In summer it was the turn of rushes and marsh plants, as 'little' or coarse hay. Rushes were plaited to make mats and baskets. Bulrushes were gathered for coopers, who used the stems between barrel staves to keep the joints watertight. Willows provided osiers for wicker baskets, eel traps, faggot bonds, etc.

The arable potential of the fens was realised in the 17th century, and a wide variety of crops were cultivated: peas, hemp, wheat, rape, oats, onions, woad, cabbages, and fruit trees being mentioned by one contemporary account. Techniques developed to manage the land. These included paring and burning, and planting cole-seed as a first crop to 'clean' reclaimed land for cultivation. As drainage became more certain, so cultivation increased. By 1800, arable had replaced pasture as the more important method of agriculture. Even rich siltland pastures around Wisbech were converted. Craddock and Walker in 1833 reported that 'nearly the whole of the grass land, excepting that in the immediate vicinity of the town, has been converted into tillage'. Market gardening was introduced, to serve the London market. Gooseberries, strawberries, raspberries, asparagus, cauliflowers and blackcurrants became firm Victorian favourites.

Arable cultivation meant further shrinkage of the peat, in some cases exposing the underlying 'buttery blue' clay. This was ironically found to enhance the water retention and therefore fertility of the soil, and many Victorian farmers laboriously transported clay from Ely to spread upon their fields.

The late Victorian depression affected fens as well as uplands. Between 1879 and 1893, the price of wheat dropped by 30 per cent and remained low until 1940. Nevertheless, the fens have been ranked among Britain's richest farmlands, far surpassing the surrounding countryside. Comparisons in 1937 showed that more men, horses and machinery were in use in the fens, and that concentration was on higher-value crops—celery (in the wetter fens), sugar-beet, and carrots,

86

onions and chicory to add variety. Pasture was and is today conspicuous by its absence.

The other great change in modern times has been the decline in water traffic. Until 1860, the ports of Ouse and Cam remained prosperous. King's Lynn was a major entrepot, with 'upland' termini at Ely, Reach, Cambridge, and St Ives. The fortunes of Wisbech fluctuated, with outfall difficulties. The arrival of the railways altered this picture drastically. Wisbech's trade halved in seven years after the opening of the St Ives line. Inland ports suffered worst, becoming no more than railway stations between the outports and London. The main beneficiary was March, arbitrarily selected as a railway marshalling centre. Today, barges have vanished and railways are vanishing, in the face of competition from juggernauts.

A fenland skater rounds a bend

A Case History

To review fen life in a few pages is to omit much. Dozens of books and booklets have been written on their character and history. The brief illustration is to examine one area in detail: a triangle in the southern fens, bounded by Wicken, Burwell, and Upware.

The history of this area is untypical, because of its 'drainage'. Burwell chose not to participate in the 18th-century drainage

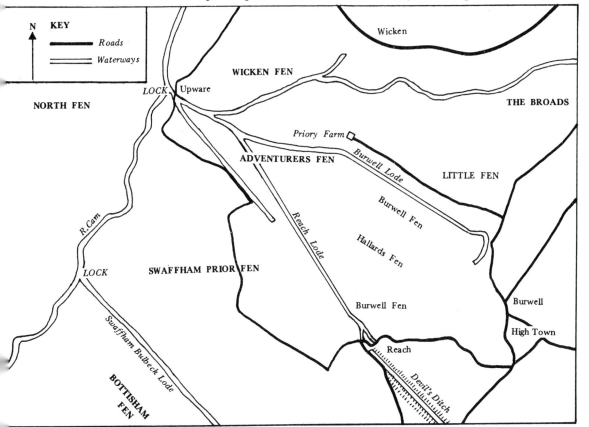

The main waterways in the Wicken, Burwell and Upware Fens.

commission established by its southern neighbours; it preferred turf-cutting and reed-cropping to arable farming. Her fens remained without drainage until 1840, when turf-cutting had reduced land levels to marsh. A Commission was established, but never prospered. It could not use the natural line of drainage, because of work done by the Bottisham and Swaffham Bulbeck Commission. Drains were instead dug to Upware and pumps established there in a vain attempt to make water run uphill. Landlords evaded drainage rates and the land remained saturated. The Commission ran into debt and could not afford to maintain the channels: a vicious, downward spiral. Some farmers had to abandon their land, or even give it away, rather than face the financial burdens which its upkeep demanded.

The result was a continuation of the traditional fen economy into modern times. The area was a delight for the Victorian naturalist, sportsman, and small boy—and for the fisherman, fowler and puntsman. Countless undergraduates spent their days here, shooting or punting. Upware became the centre of their activities. In the middle of the 19th century there were three boating inns in the hamlet, including the *Lord Nelson*—better known from its sign as the 'Five Miles From Anywhere—No Hurry!' Here was founded the Upware Republic Society, its members including famous names of the future, like Samuel Butler. The Bustle was Upware's annual fair—with dancing booths, skittle alleys, and prizes for various alcoholic feats devised by Richard Fielder of Jesus College. The 1862 Bustle became a rolling fight between local men, undergraduates and strangers from surrounding villages, during which the police were thrown into the river. Fielder went on to higher things, proclaiming himself king of Upware and challenging all to dispute his sovereignty. It was a last moment of glory; the hamlet declined rapidly into a literal backwater after the construction of the railways.

Neglect continued in the Burwell fens. Each year, less land was cultivated. The spread of fen plants—mint, orchid, bedstraw, vetch, thistle—made it a haven for rare butterflies and moths, including the swallowtail, and for a mass of birdlife varying in size from the sedge-warbler to the bittern and marsh harrier. Wicken Fen and neighbouring Adventurers' Fen became nature reserves, the farmland about remaining 'a waterlogged jungle of litter, reeds and sedge'. After flooding in the 1930s, the fen deteriorated even further.

It was then that an aspiring horticulturist, Alan Bloom, bought Priory Farm amid this wilderness. His intention was to become a proper fen farmer, yet prospects seemed bleak. The farm was all but derelict; approached only by a grass drove, with few intact buildings and fewer drains. The land was full of 'bog oaks'—gigantic tree stumps

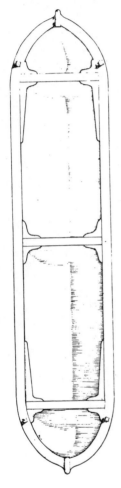

Outline plan of a fen lighter

88

24. (*right*) The most famous wind-mill in Cambridgeshire stands today at Wicken Fen. It is a marsh mill of smock type, built on brick, and formerly stood in neighbouring Adventurer's Fen.

25. (*below*) A winter view of the Engine House at Stretham, on the Great Ouse. The steam pump is preserved by a Trust, and open to members of the public. The House and Engine alike date from the earliest days of steam drainage, *c.*1830.

26. The 'hard way': a gang of men 'slubs out' a drain near Prickwillow, in the 1890s. Note the windmill in the distance and the men's dress.

27. A steam bucket dredger at work in the Cambridgeshire lodes at the very end of the 19th century.

28.   Threshing at Soham in the 1890s. The farmer's wife and children have come out to be in the picture; the men and boys keep on working.

29.   A turn-of-the-century view of Reach Green from the north-west end of Devil's Dyke. The Green housed Reach's famous medieval Fairs. Beyond the flagpole and trees lies The Hythe—Reach's harbour area.

30. Wicken Fen windmill—sole survivor of the thousands once used to drain the fens.

30A. The Stretham Engine House: for fen drainage engine.

rotted by prehistoric flooding. Terrible to extract, they were worthless, even as firewood. His first crop, of mustard, failed, and attempts to ditch the land failed in the appalling winter of 1940. The farm looked doomed. It was the war which saved Bloom, and the Burwell fens. A campaign was launched to reclaim all waste fenlands. The Great Ouse Catchment Board dissolved the defunct Burwell Drainage Commission and started draining the area themselves. They cut a drain under Burwell and Reach Lodes into Swaffham Lode, restoring the natural line of drainage. Fen droves were concreted. The National Trust was 'persuaded' to relinquish Adventurers' Fen for cultivation. Naturalists protested, in vain: 'They drained the fen with a great clamour of bureaucratic self-praise. The waters went away and the fish died by the cartload. The reeds stood rustling and dry above the black mud. Then they set fire to the reeds, and for a day or two my secret fen roared and crackled in a tawny yellow, red-hot sea of flame' (J. W. Day).

The Old Fen at Wicken, at the turn of the century.

Bloom's struggles to farm this land were heroic and were rewarded eventually when royalty visited Priory Farm. Yet Adventurers' Fen was his only upon loan, and was returned to the Trust after the war, against Bloom's bitter pleas. Today, it forms part of the great reserve at Wicken Fen. The main reserve with its wildlife, windmill and barges shows the stages by which half-drained fen will grow out into wooded 'carr'. Adventurers' Fen and mere is by contrast a true wasteland, with even more varied birdlife. Next door is Priory Farm, one of few fenland farms given partly to pasture—for this is still wetland, and even now not entirely reclaimed.

The Cathedral and City of Ely

IX The New Agriculture and the Old Problems

THE NEW AGRICULTURE

An Agrarian Revolution

Between 1700 and 1900, there was a revolution in agriculture, in Cambridgeshire as elsewhere. It was not a revolution in rural society—the three classes of landowner, yeoman farmer, and landless labourer that had emerged by 1700 continued to predominate. The changes were in agriculture itself. Of these, the greatest was the completion of enclosure. Open fields survived late in the county, despite piecemeal enclosures between 1300 and 1700. Of the uplands' 147,000 arable acres in 1800, 132,000 remained in open, strip-divided fields. This survival gave Cambridgeshire an unenviable, primitive reputation, 'the Bœotia of agriculture'. The general prosperity of 18th-century farming postponed, but could not prevent enclosure. The immediate spur came in 1794 from an American agriculturalist, Charles Vancouver. In a report to the national Board of Agriculture, Vancouver attacked Cambridgeshire's open fields as uneconomic and wasteful. Local farmers who disagreed were 'flock-masters . . . the mass of the farmers are decidedly for the measure'. Enclosure meant increased population, higher employment, security of tenure for tenant farmers—and fat profits. He was swimming with an existing tide. The first Act for enclosure of a Cambridgeshire parish was in 1770. Three others had succumbed by 1794, including Chippenham, where eight enclosed farms had replaced a jumble of common fields and fens. The report accelerated the process. By 1811, almost 50 per cent of the land had been enclosed. William Gooch in his own survey applauded the results, citing increased yields and land values, but the changeover was gradual. In 1830, William Cobbett could still describe the transition:

> Immediately upon quitting Royston, you come along, for a considerable distance, with enclosed fields on the left and open common fields on the right. The fields on the left seem to have been enclosed by Act of Parliament, and they certainly are the most beautiful tract of fields that I ever saw.

Twenty-six Enclosure Acts followed, and a General Act in 1836. Most remaining open fields vanished before 1850, but Hildersham remained common until the 1880s, and Soham still has open fields.

A Cambridgeshire corn dolly

91

Enclosure transformed the physical appearance of Cambridgeshire. Plains of open fields gave way to large, hedged fields. Myriad winding tracks were replaced by long, green lanes ironically given ancient names on maps, such as the Street and Icknield Ways. Village greens were enclosed at Kingston, Willingham and Shelford. Beauty and common rights bowed before agricultural efficiency.

Enclosure was accompanied by changes in farming techniques. Upland farming in the 18th century remained mixed, with pasture much in evidence. The chalklands in particular were a place for sheep, predominantly the Norfolk, West Country and native Cambridgeshire breeds. Parishes like Swaffham Bulbeck used elaborate drainage systems with moats and sluices to create lush water-meadows. Cattle were rarer, mixed indiscriminately with arable, interfering with good husbandry. One exception was 'the Dairies', around Shingay, Wendy and Whaddon. The principal arable crops in the 18th century were saffron, in the far south, and barley. The latter went to Ware and Royston for malt production. Saffron gradually disappeared as a main crop, barley and other grains increasing production at the expense of pasture. The demands of a growing population for bread coincided with new crop rotation systems and farm machinery to produce enormously higher yields. The heyday of Cambridgeshire farming was 1840–75, before cheap American and Canadian corn brought competition and depression.

A barley kosher or hummeller

The Victorian county was also a place of industry, based on farming needs. Cambridgeshire's oddest industry was coprolite-digging—the extraction of phosphatised clay nodules for fertiliser. Coprolites occurred in a belt from Soham to Barrington and were exhausted in a rush between 1850 and 1890. It was an industry unique in England. Nodules were excavated in trenches, yielding 300 tons an acre. Other mineral industries were for the building trade. Carstone and clunch were quarried into the 20th century; brickworks dotted the fen clays; and cement works were established at Shepreth, Meldreth, and Barrington. The growth of woad for dyeing continued until 1914 at Parson's Drove. Woad leaves were plucked, crushed, balled and fermented, using horse-drawn grinding wheels, drying shelves and 'couching houses'. Workmen laboured in total darkness amid a foul, clinging stench. Straw-plaiting for bowler hats was done at Little Shelford and Little Gransden. Timber was worked at Wisbech, where everything from chip-baskets and gateposts to railway sleepers and telegraph poles was made. There were two paper factories at Sawston. These survive today, as does the greatest industry of them all—the making, bottling, and canning of jam, at the Chivers' factory in Histon. Established in 1873, by 1930 it employed 3,000 people.

General and heavy industry were, however, scarce, even in Cambridge and the larger towns. It was an agricultural county.

Prosperity for Some

The wealth of 18th-century landowners is reflected in a rash of new buildings. The most famous country house of this period is Wimpole Hall. Built in the 17th century by Sir Thomas Chichele, it was progressively enlarged in the 18th century by the Earls of Oxford and Hardwicke. Its magnificent parklands include work by Bridgeman, Capability Brown, and Repton, and included an imposing two-mile avenue of elms recently removed, and a surviving 'Gothick Ruin'. The house remains testimony to the wealth of the aristocracy, and was opened to the public by the National Trust. Wimpole was only the greatest of a dozen period mansions. Manors at Brinkley and Stetchworth, halls at Childerley, Gamlingay, and Shepreth demonstrate the gentry's confidence. Chippenham Hall was emparked by Lord Orford, after purchasing and demolishing cottages in the village. Similar clearances for landscaping took place at Madingley, Croxton and Wimpole itself. The humps and hollows by Wimpole church are the marks left after the removal of one village; a second was destroyed to construct the southern avenue. Only a single terrrace built by the Hardwickes in Victorian times remains of a once thriving community. It was an age in which landowners wielded almost unlimited influence.

This power is never clearer than in Cambridgeshire politics. Before 1740, political life depended on minor gentry, who filled the offices of J.P.s and M.P.s. The Cottons, Peytons, Cutts, and later Harleys and Shepherds contended for control under arbitrary Whig and Tory affiliations. This picture changed abruptly after the arrival of genuine aristocrats: Wimpole was bought by the Earl of Hardwicke; and Cheveley by John Manners, Marquess of Granby, son of the Duke of Rutland. The Hardwickes and the Rutlands controlled county elections for 150 years. Sometimes they compromised, each taking one of the two parliamentary seats. Between 1770 and 1780, they competed furiously for a monopoly. For long, Hardwicke dominance in Cambridgeshire was matched by Rutland dominance in the city of Cambridge. The 1832 Reform Bill only confirmed their position; a Hardwicke was returned solidly in 1878, and was usually accompanied by a Rutland. Wimpole meanwhile became the epicentre of high Victorian society.

Much less is known about the lesser landowners, squires and farmers. It was an age of 'squarsons', parson squires owning most of their parishes. Large 19th-century rectories and extensive Victorian

Contemporary drawing of the Folly in the grounds of Wimpole House.

'restoration' within our churches bear testimony to their influence. The frills, fancies and furniture associated with Victoriana belonged in country areas only to the squirearchy, farmers and tradesmen. Their prosperity varied greatly with fluctuations in the economy. In good times, they prospered, and could be seen at the Newmarket races. Generally, they grumbled, blaming the government, the weather, their workers. When times were really bad, the sackings started.

THE OLD PROBLEMS

Poverty for Others

> It is obvious that the labourer's earnings are no more than shall keep him merely in existence, and when deductions are made for house-rent, firing, etc, his income is not equal to what is allowed for a felon!

The conversion of the peasantry into landless labourers did not inevitably mean poverty. In the good years before 1780, labourers fared reasonably well, sharing in part the prosperity of their superiors. Lack of land, however, made them dependent upon work and wages. No longer could bad times be ridden out on the strength of the home acres, or the strips in open fields.

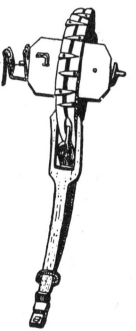

After 1750, population began to grow, accelerating in the 19th century to reach an 80 per cent rise in four decades, and Melbourn, for example, more than doubled in size. More mouths meant high food prices, more hands kept wages low. In 1794, Vancouver recorded averages wages of 9s. a week for rural labourers. This rose to about 13s. during the period of greater Victorian prosperity, but had fallen back to 10s. by 1890. The extra shilling could not compensate for inflation. This poverty necessarily depressed other dependent tradesmen such as the shopkeeper, cobbler, or publican. Below the employed labourer, however, lay the workless, fluctuating in number. In Melbourn, in 1834, the unemployment rate was 33 per cent and rising. Destitution and workhouse loomed.

It was an age of large families. A man and wife might have eight children, raising three or four. Feeding these in infancy was a financial burden, restricting the woman's paid labour in the fields. (Her casual labour might earn £2 a year, a vital supplement to his wages.) Children were put to work from the age of eight on various farm jobs, mostly paying their way into adolescence. A large family was an investment, the children eventually becoming the supporters of their parents' dotage.

An 18th-century mantrap

Food was scarce. Reverend Yorke records his parishioners' meals in the good years after 1850: a midday meal of boiled cabbage and

95

A Cambridgeshire wagon with high sides

home-fatted bacon; bread and cheese as staples; and butcher's meat on Sunday only. Potatoes and vegetables from the cottage-garden supplemented the diet. Villagers' favourite celebration was understandably the feast, when tables groaned with meats, pies, soups and unheard-of delicacies. The only other luxury was beer—drunk by the man only, when he could afford it, and then in quantity. The number of alehouses would stagger today's villager: five in a single street in Burwell; and one for the dozen cottages in New Wimpole.

Clothing reflected poverty. Victorian farmworkers dressed in fustian or moleskin trousers, with braces, a collarless shirt buttoned to the neck, and a flat hat. Some still wore the home-made clothes of former generations: the smock, worsted stockings, and yellow gaiters. Women wore plain, print dresses, and lindsey-woolseys. Children would be in hand-me-downs and habitually went barefoot. Many families were required by employers to attend church, perforce acquiring a set of 'best' clothes—jacket and trousers for the man, and a patterned or bordered dress for his wife. These appeared only on Sundays, feasts, marriages and deaths.

Housing conditions varied. The neat estate houses at New Wimpole were luxurious in comparison to nearby Melbourn. There, all but 30 of 200 houses were shared. The *Morning Chronicle* in 1850 described one house containing 13 families! Traditional building materials were clunch and clay bat, under a thatch, tile or slate roof. Constructing such a house could cost £15; and with rent at 2s. a week, this was soon recovered. Families with more than two rooms were counted fortunate, and indoor sanitation was non-existent. Furniture would comprise a stump bed, a table, some wooden chairs, a sink, and rush matting. Samplers and stitched mottoes served as the principal wall decorations for most peasants. Books were limited to a family Bible, perhaps an almanack or sermon. Lighting was by candles.

Life was precarious. The average age of death was 33 in the early 19th century as infant mortality was so high. Tuberculosis, influenza, malaria and other fevers raged, as medicines were outside the family purse. The same *Morning Chronicle* reporter recorded a house in Witchford containing two families. In one room lay a family stricken by typhoid; next door, two sisters were dying of typhus. Cholera arrived in 1830, taking a terrible toll:

> In memory of 67 individuals of various age and either sex who in the short period from June 21st to August 13th A.D. 1832 Died in this Rectory of Asiatic Cholera, a frightful and previously unknown disease in this country. Reader, why hast thou been spared? To what purpose hast thou been left until now?—Memorial, Upware church.

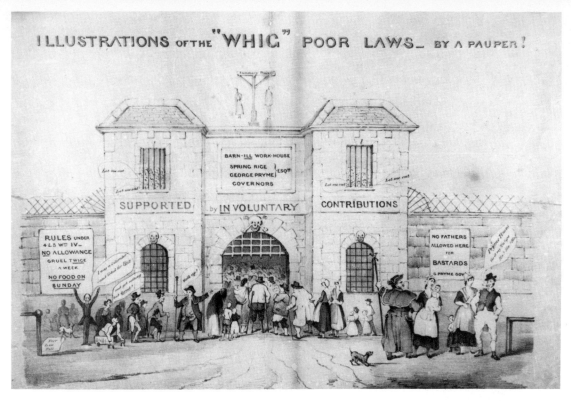

31. The Tories made much capital out of the Liberals' support for the 1834 Poor Law Amendment Act: pictured here is Barnwell Workhouse, in a contemporary cartoon. George Pryme was Liberal MP for Cambridge.

32. Order, patriotism and poverty prevail in this photograph of Chesterton preparatory school, taken just before the First World War.

33. Typical thatched peasant cottages with external water supply at Abington early in the 20th century. Picturesque, but poor!

34. A village scene taken at Dry Drayton as late as 1929 shows how long rural poverty lasted in Cambridgeshire. Briscoe (bottom left) was the Tory candidate.

35. Warehouses and commercial buildings crowd the riverbanks at Wisbech, in the first quarter of this century. The trading fortunes of the town rose and fell as the river silted up and was drained clear.

36. The opening of Cambridge Station in 1845 depicted by a contemporary artist. The fine classical facing of the station is as noticeable as the primitive rolling stock.

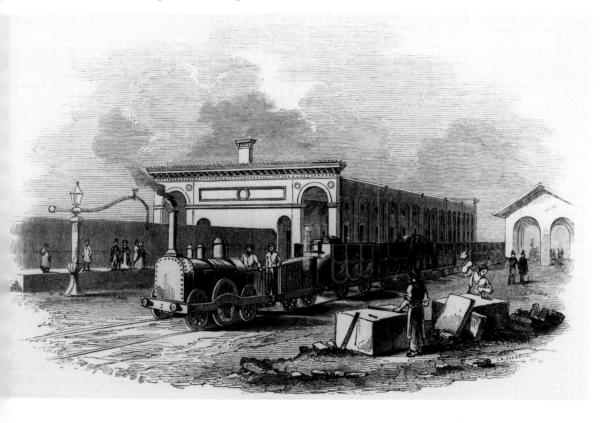

37. March became a major centre of the railways; an East Anglian Crewe. The station is here pictured at the height of its importance, *c.*1910.

38. The deserted Victorian station at Swaffham Prior testifies to the arrival and departure of the railways in Cambridgeshire. It stood originally on the Cambridge-Burwell-Mildenhall line.

Better sanitation and cheaper medicines gradually reduced disease, but poorer housing conditions kept certain villages as haunts of death. Mary Chamberlain's *Fenwomen* describes families in pits at Hilgay. A doctor in 1853 reported the same in Soham, noting 500 people in a single pit—'in a state of great deprivation and dirty in the extreme'.

John Board, from Swavesey, led a typical life. In his childhood, he caught scarlet fever and went lame. This hampered his work, driving horses for ploughmen, and brought frequent floggings. His wages aged 15 were 4s. a week for the same heavy labour as adult workers. Not until he was 24 did he have enough money to marry. 'As Regards our Household stuf we had very Little true I had a bed and I had a very good Family Bible and I had . . . 3s.'. He and his wife lived a year with his parents, accumulating some bits, including a baby. John's desire to keep what little status he had even prevented close relations with his wife. 'I felt as if I Dare not tell her how much I Loved her because I thought she Would be trespising on were I shold be and that would be the Head of the House'. The house was two rooms between a blacksmith and a cobbler, with hammering on either side for 18 hours a day. They had three more children, two dying. John broke his collar-bone at work, was laid up for six weeks, then obtained only casual work and fell into debt. The house burned down, forcing them into hired rooms at the inn. His life was a struggle for subsistence; yet even in widowerhood and destitution, he told his story with humour, not self-pity. After all, he had had a job.

A straw plait or splint mill

Workhouses and Schools

For the disease of unemployment, there were two cures: the palliative of poor relief, and the preventative of education.

From 1700 to 1834, poor relief was based on Elizabethan Poor Laws. These established the parish as the unit of relief, appointed overseers for each parish, and ordered the removal of destitute strangers to their native parish. The principles were 'Instruction for youth, employment for the healthy, comfort for the aged and infirm, reform for the profligate'. This meant the forced apprenticeship of children, poor houses for the helpless, workhouses for the able-bodied, and Houses of Correction for the 'deliberately' idle.

During the 18th century this system failed due to population pressure. Wisbech had great initial success with its workhouse, built in 1722 to accommodate 80 paupers. Brewing, baking and spinning were the main work; the master was paid a fixed salary, and inmates received a good basic diet. This type of workhouse was adopted in other fenland towns such as Ely, Littleport, Soham and Chatteris.

Linton and Royston built Houses of Correction and Work to cope with the flood of vagrants along Icknield Way and Ermine Street. Cambridge adopted parochial workhouses, after the failure of a corporate scheme in 1727. After 1770, however, increasing population and deepening recession inflated the numbers who needed relief. The cost of relief rose from £1½m. to £7m. by 1831. Existing workhouses were inadequate and constructing others would have been more expensive. One expedient was the Speenhamland System, where labourers who earned below a certain level received supplements from the public rate, and the unemployed were set to public works. This failed. It depressed real wages, demoralising the poor. By 1825, Cambridgeshire was the tenth highest spender among counties on poor relief, yet suffered riots of the unemployed at Sawston and Kirtling.

The result was the Poor Law Act of 1834, which abolished the Speenhamland System and ruled that relief would be available only within workhouses. Parishes were combined into unions under elected Boards of Guardians, to erect workhouses upon the public rates. Their living conditions would be below anything available outside, to encourage paupers to find work—in times of chronic unemployment! The Act was passed as a 'humanitarian' measure, that would also reduce public rates. It did the latter—by 30 per cent in Cambridgeshire. Its humanitarianism is another matter. Even Guardians sometimes petitioned for some form of outdoor relief for the able-bodied, if only during harvests, but they were denied. Workhouses were built, officials appointed: a master, matron, schoolteacher, chaplain, medical officer, and nurse for each house. The nine houses in Cambridgeshire reflected a central model, with plain, prison-like exteriors and institutional design. Men, women and children were segregated, as were the able-bodied and infirm. Able-bodied paupers over seven worked a ten-hour day with Sundays off. The day began at 5.00 a.m. (7.00 a.m. in winter), continuing until lights out at 8.00 p.m. Women cleaned the workhouse, cooked food, laundered, tended the sick and infants, and made workhouse uniforms. Boys and girls knitted. Men were given hard, degrading labour, picking oakum and grinding bones. Food was sufficient, but monotonous, and ale forbidden. Fear of the workhouse grew—but for the unemployed, there was no alternative.

Education after 1700 depended upon endowed schools and Sunday schools. The S.P.C.K. founded 37 endowed schools in Cambridgeshire, the first in 1704 in Cambridge itself. Their aims were limited. No pupil stayed more than three years, and the only subjects taught were reading, writing, arithmetic, and psalm-singing. Other schools were established by legacies in wills, often of leading Dissenters. By 1787, half of Cambridgeshire's parishes had some elementary school, usually

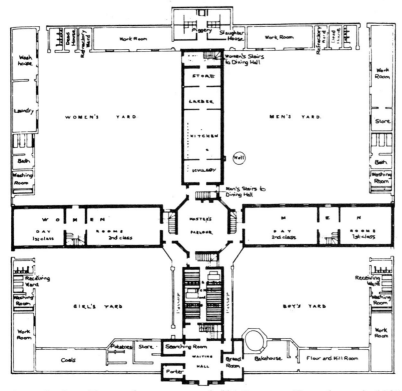

A standard workhouse plan recommended by Sampson Kempthorne in 1835.

free. The proportion reached 75 per cent by 1800. It was, however, the farmers' and tradesmen's children who really benefited. Two-thirds of all children remained entirely without schooling. The development of Sunday schools after 1785 was designed partly to meet this need. Richard Watson, archdeacon of Ely, was active in the movement, despite opposition from other Anglicans who feared protest by an educated peasantry.

The 19th century saw more charity schools, but also the first state education. After 1833, Liberal governments gave increasing support to schooling and by 1867, 66 elementary schools with 12,000 children in Cambridgeshire received state aid. The 1870 Education Act established universal, free and compulsory elementary education. Subsequent legislation on child labour increased attendance; ignorance and illiteracy began to decrease, and with them a few of the absolute class differences of rural Cambridgeshire. It was a slow process.

PROTEST AND RIOT

'Bread or Blood'!

With poverty came protest—and with protest, riot. The prosperity of the 18th century had meant peace in the fields of upland Cambridgeshire, and only occasional disturbances in the turbulent fens. This changed with recession. The 1790s saw bread riots, and societies in Cambridge commemorating the French Revolution. The main, ineffectual protests of this period were against enclosure, and these continued for decades. Gooch and Young tempered enthusiasm for enclosure with warnings about the damage to common rights. At Guilden Morden, 'The poor are greatly alarmed and view the steps taken for enclosure with terror'. Chippenham reacted to enclosure first by legal action and then invasion of the fen closes. Hedge-breaking continued sporadically throughout the period.

It was in the years after Waterloo that protest began in earnest, due mostly to the price of corn. Isolation from Continental wheatfields during wartime had created high demand and high prices. Bread was expensive, but labourers had work. The end of war and importation of foreign wheat slashed prices and wages. Bread was cheap, but still beyond the purse of many. Even worse, many were made jobless, joined in unemployment by returning soldiers. Farmers reacted by demanding protection from imports, and the repeal of property taxes. Mobilising their labourers in support they held mass rallies, which were sometimes violent. These were successful; the Corn Laws were passed and income tax repealed. This did not benefit the poor; protection brought high bread prices, without increasing employment or wages.

A fiddle and bow for scattering seeds

Protest was sporadic throughout East Anglia. It began with attacks on farm property in isolated villages in 1816, then spread to personal assaults and town riots. Bury St Edmunds, Brandon, Norwich and Downham Market were all affected. The demand was for cheap bread, 'Bread or Blood'. By May 1816, a loaf cost 11¾d., and a quartern of wheat had risen 18s. in three weeks. Bread was too dear for the poor.

On 22 May in Littleport 60 labourers met in the *Globe* inn, waiting for the arrival of Southery and Denver men involved in earlier riots. When these did not arrive, the 60 decided on immediate action. Their first targets were two unpopular landowners, Henry Martin and the vicar, John Vadell. Forced to parley, these two offered concessions, including cheap flour and wage rises. Riots exploded later that evening, fed by drink and fears that these concessions would not be honoured. Farmhouses were ransacked and their owners robbed. A march was proclaimed to Ely, to get confirmation of the promises from local magistrates. It occurred the next day, under direction of former soldiers. Pitchforks became pikes, shotguns muskets, a punt gun on a cart served for artillery. Their demands now included cheap beer and a pardon, and they massed in Ely market. Under threat of force, the magistrates consented. Most of the train then returned to Littleport, a few staying to sack shops and houses.

DESCRIPTION of TWO MEN

detected in the act of **SETTING FIRE** to a **STACK of OATS** in the Parish of **PAMPISFORD**, in the County of Cambridge, about **Eight o'clock** in the evening of **MONDAY** the **6th** of *December*, **1830.**

One a tall Man, about 5 feet 10 in. high, sandy whiskers, large red nose, apparently between 50 and 60 years of age. Wore at the time a snuff-colored straight coat, light-colored pantaloons, and low shoes.

The other Man was apparently about 5 feet 4 inches, and between 30 and 40 years of age; had large black full whiskers, extending under the chin. He wore a blue straight coat, light colored breeches, and boots with cloth overall-tops.

Both the Men were seen at Pampisford at half-past twelve at noon on Monday, coming from Babraham, and probably from the New-market road.

HODSON, PRINTER, CAMBRIDGE.

A typical account of 'Captain Swing' at work, 6 Dec. 1830 (from a copy in the Cambridgeshire Collection).

The authorities' concessions were only delaying tactics, however, and they acted quickly to suppress the threat. On 24 May there was a counter-attack by cavalry under Sir Henry Bate Dudley. The rioters had barricaded themselves inside the *George,* and put up armed resistance. Three soldiers were injured and two labourers killed before restoration of order. Nearly a hundred arrests were made. Many fled across the fens and were rounded up over a fortnight by Bow Street Runners and armed cavalry. The rioters were tried at Ely and sentenced harshly. Nineteen death sentences were eventually commuted to transportation, but five men were hanged on 28 June. Public opinion had turned in favour of the condemned and a rope and cart were obtained only with great difficulty. It was severe punishment for mere robbery, and did not prevent further protest, including an incipient riot at Wisbech. As late as 1819, there were riotous proclamations in Coveney, but gradually the threat of violence subsided . . . temporarily.

Design from a butter stamp

'Captain Swing' and the Reverend Moberley

The Littleport Riots are famous, but violence continued throughout the early 19th century. Particular targets of discontent were the Poor Laws, and the introduction of farm machinery.

Workhouses were a target even before the 1834 Act. Two of the worst affrays were at Bassingbourn in 1832, and at Royston three years later. A house at Linton was delayed by threats of arson; once built, it was attacked, and windows smashed. Such casual violence did not, however, seriously challenge the Poor Laws. In 1836, a concerted campaign began, led by the Reverend F. H. Moberley, of Kingston. Moberley called the Act 'tyrannical, unconstitutional, anti-scriptural, anti-Christian, unnatural, cruel and impolitic'. It degraded workers, inciting them to crime as an alternative to the workhouse. Separation of men and women inside its doors destroyed the family, encouraging promiscuity and—worse still—homosexuality. Public meetings were held throughout Cambridgeshire. The authorities put pressure on Moberley; not merely the Earl of Hardwicke, Lord Lieutenant of Cambridgeshire, but the Home Secretary, Lord John Russell, and Moberley's superior, the Bishop of Ely threatened him with disfavour. The campaign was ineffective. A petition of 35,000 signatures was sent in—and ignored. Protest continued after 1837, but never impeded the implementation of the Act.

It was an age of rural violence—of 'Captain Swing', a mythical leader whose real followers fired hayricks and houses, smashed farm machinery and sent threatening letters. Demands for an end to tithes

102

gained sympathies from similarly burdened farmers, but labourers also wanted wage increases, and to stop the installation of more threshing-machines. The latter were removing much of the landworkers' precarious winter employment. The movement in Cambridgeshire concentrated on arson, beginning in November 1830 with a series of conflagrations—in Coveney, Willingham, Coton, Pampisford, Chatteris and March. There were riots at Balsham, Horseheath, and Abington Piggotts, machine-breakings at Croydon, and sheep-stealing at Whittlesey. Convicted men were treated severely, two incendiarists were hanged for firing ricks. Waterbeach, Eaton Socon and Soham were fired repeatedly, while in 1846 no fewer than 12 men were charged in a single assize at March with sheep-stealing. Cambridgeshire foolishly resisted the introduction of a police force; and when village police were finally appointed, they were far from safe. One constable at Cheveley was attacked by sheep-stealers, others murdered at Burwell and Hilgay. The 'respectable' created Protection Associations, offering high rewards for information about miscreants, but villagers hid their own and punished informers mercilessly.

This violence shows the extremes to which labourers had to go to influence their condition. Political or union activity was impossible without the vote or legal sanction for collective bargaining. All non-violent opportunities were eagerly taken up. The short-lived Grand National Consolidated Trade Union had an active Cambridgeshire branch in the 1830s; the Chartists were equally busy in the fens after 1837. One experiment sought to bypass conventional politics entirely. The socialist Robert Owen started a commune in Manea Fen, at Colony Farm. Designed in 1838 as a 200-acre co-operative under the motto 'Each for All', it was an ambitious project serving as a model for labourers elsewhere. Colonists erected buildings, organised recreation and education, and worked the land communally for vouchers redeemable at the community store. A newsletter was produced, and widely distributed. Under-financed, beset with drainage problems, the 'Cambridgeshire Community Number One' also harboured internal dissension. The leader, William Hodson of Upwell, eventually resigned. Others followed, and the community was dead by 1851.

'Unionise'

The following two decades saw relatively little protest. Earlier failures and the comparative prosperity of mid-Victorian agriculture brought peace to Cambridgeshire. Resentment, however, simmered; and legal changes in 1871 by the incoming Liberal government brought it to the surface.

The change was the limited recognition given to the right to form trade unions. The result was a series of 'agricultural welfare societies'. The movement entered Cambridgeshire in 1872, with meetings throughout the county. Some were content merely with a threat to unionise; a meeting of 200 labourers at Guyhirn produced instant wage rises. The first union to develop, the South Cambridgeshire Agricultural Labourers' Society, followed a gathering of 1,500 workers from Duxford and Sawston, reported by the *Daily News*. 'Speaker after speaker came forward and dilated on the hardship of living on 1s. 8d. a day.' One speaker demanded shorter hours and was immediately sacked by his employer. The Society gained many quick victories. Branches were established in villages throughout the uplands, similar associations arising in the northern fens. Local unions participated in the Conference at Leamington Spa, merging with Joseph Arch's National Agricultural Labourers' Union. Strikes proved the power of communal labour, and won concessions.

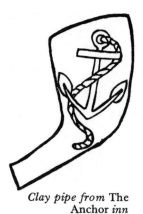

Clay pipe from The Anchor *inn*

A counter-attack was inevitable. Mobs were raised to disrupt union meetings. Organisers were sacked, and strikers locked out. Farmers reduced wages during slack periods, and replaced striking workers with child labour, Irish blacklegs, or farm machinery. Many prosecuted unionists under the Master and Servant Act or a range of bye-laws. One widow at Cherry Hinton had her parish relief withdrawn when her son joined the union. 'Farmers Defence Associations' were formed at Newmarket and Ely, and they agreed to employ no unionists, nor to pay more than 13s. a week. The disputes had strong political and religious overtones. Support for the unions came from the Liberal Party and Dissenter clergy. The Tories and Church of England as resolutely opposed change. Existing disputes over housing, charity lands, etc., helped to make some villages, such as Exning, Cottenham and Sawston, centres of unionism.

The National Agricultural Labourers' Union failed. A comprehensive lock-out by the Newmarket Farmers' Defence Association broke it financially, forcing a general reduction in wages. The onset of depression after 1875 hit the budget and morale of the labourers. Emigration to New Zealand and Canada, a feature of Cambridgeshire life since the 1840s, reached new heights. The long-term picture proved rather better. N.A.L.U. nationally survived, becoming the National Union of Agricultural and Allied Workers. Today, N.U.A.W. is part of the T.G.W.U., the biggest union in Britain.

T.G.W.U. has a rest home in the Cambridgeshire fens. Appropriately, it is at Littleport. It is as good a memorial to the five dead after the Riots as they could, perhaps, have wished.

THE TWENTIETH CENTURY

The changes in rural Cambridgeshire during the last 80 years would require an entire chapter to cover. It is, however, possible to examine the main themes of this chapter, extended into modern times.

The county remains overwhelmingly a rural area, devoted to agriculture. It has suffered in hard times, e.g., between the wars, and prospered in wartime and during the post-war population explosion. The use of fertilisers, chemicals and machinery has immeasurably increased, with a corresponding reduction in the farm work force. The main upland cash crops are wheat, barley, sugar-beet and potatoes. Livestock and animal fodder crops (turnips, swedes, oats, mangolds) have declined. Only pigs and chickens have increased in number, due to battery farming. Farms have got larger, through amalgamation. The combine harvester has created an open, hedgeless landscape almost resembling the common fields before enclosure. Cambridgeshire is an agricultural factory.

The reduction of the rural work force and introduction of mechnisation has increased the status of the farm labourer, but he or she remains among the poorest-paid of workers. The rapid growth of welfare facilities has considerably eased working-class life. The Poor Law and workhouses survived, incredibly, until 1948, despite criticism from Royal Commissions and all party politicians. Their function was, however, increasingly undermined by specific welfare measures: school meals; medical inspections; old-age pensions; unemployment insurance; and labour exchanges. Today, we operate 'outdoor relief' through social security and dole. Free, compulsory education has created a more mobile society. Cambridgeshire's own special contribution has been the village college, combining secondary school and community centre in a single building serving several villages. The invasion of the villages by car-owning workers from Cambridge has accelerated progress in education, and reduced the dominance of local farmers over rural communities. Politically the county remains predominantly Conservative, as it has done throughout the 100 years of householder suffrage. The Isle of Ely is, however, at the moment of writing, once more a Liberal seat.

X A University City: Cambridge 1680-1900

THE UNIVERSITY

Genius, Stagnation and Repression

Carved bookcase end from Clare College (18th century)

Eighteenth-century Cambridge scholarship was dominated by the shadows of two men: Sir Isaac Newton and Richard Bentley. Newton's origins were humble and he entered Trinity in 1661 as a sub-sizar or common student. His training was under Cambridge's first great mathematician, Isaac Burrow, whom he succeeded as Fellow of Trinity in 1667 at the age of twenty-five. His universal theories of gravity and *Principia Mathematica* (1687) elevated him into the position of England's most eminent scientist. Newton worked actively for the university, resisting James II's imposition of Catholic Fellows and Masters. He also inspired numerous lesser figures—such as Roger Cotes, William Whiston, and Astronomer-Royal John Flamsteed. The growth of anatomical studies under Rolfe, Hales and Stukeley was matched in botany by John Ray and in chemistry by Vigani. Their successes owed much to the intellectual atmosphere created by Newton.

Richard Bentley, also of Trinity, is a contrasting figure. England's greatest classical scholar, he is remembered less for his scholarship than for bitter collegiate controversy. As Master, Bentley ordered expensive additions to his Lodge and the Chapel, raising his salary at the expense of other Fellows. Years of legal dispute dragged on after 1711, preventing Bentley from establishing classics as a major university discipline. The result was that mathematics, before 1660 only one subject among many, became in 1730 practically the only subject that mattered. Students were officially examined in philosophy, classics and divinity. Divinity tuition was very patchy, despite four professors of theology. Equally little attention was given to classics. An undergraduate could leave entirely ignorant of Tacitus, Lucretius, Aeschylus, Plato, or Aristotle, with only just enough Latin to survive the oral 'Disputationes'. As these gave way to written 'Tripos' examinations, so classics became a further backwater relieved only by special competitions for Greek odes, Latin epigrams, etc. 'Philosophy' meant mathematics, and mathematics meant Euclid and Newton. Students were rigidly graded into Wranglers, senior and Junior Optimes, and Wranglers were listed in order of merit. Competition

106

to become First Wrangler was intense, likely candidates resorting to private tuition to boost their chances. Tutors marking examinations were accused of favouritism towards their own pupils, not without reason.

The emphasis on mathematics harmed other subjects. Many students with genius in other fields perforce left Cambridge with a poor honours or ordinary degree. Civil and common law languished. There were no distinguished professors in physic or anatomy. The chairs of Greek, Hebrew, Moral Philosophy, History and Modern Languages were all sinecures. Botany flourished temporarily, with annual courses after 1763, until the election of a non-resident professor. Chemistry alone blossomed, under vigorous scholars like Watson, Farish, and Milner. But examinations almost ignored chemistry, and few students were therefore interested. In mathematics itself, the concentration on Newton prevented original research; the Plumian and Lucasian chairs, and the Lowndean chair of Astronomy and Geometry attracted few major scholars. Thus research stagnated.

An 18th-century undergraduate

The average undergraduate's life bore little resemblance to the few struggling to become First Wrangler. It was a century in which numbers and interest declined. Four hundred and fifty annual matriculations in the 17th century declined to 150, the biggest fall being in the numbers of poor scholars or sizars. More aristocratic students generally eschewed scholarship, taking ordinary degrees after sedulous professional 'cramming'—as Cowper wrote,

> Proceeding soon a graduated dunce . . .
> And he was competent whose purse was so.

Relatives of nobility and royalty received degrees without being examined at all! The number of degrees awarded declined annually to 1775, when only 75 graduations took place.

> We sauntered, played, or rioted; we talked
> Unprofitable talk at morning hours;
> Drifted about along the streets and walks,
> Read lazily in trivial books, went forth
> To gallop through the country in blind zeal
> Of senseless horsemanship, or on the breast
> Of Cam sailed boisterously . . .

A College servant

Wordsworth's lines from *The Prelude* aptly sum up his and many other students' lives in Cambridge: gambling; drinking; whoring; talking in coffee shops. Like Gray, he burgeoned as a poet only after graduation. Academics set a generally poor example. Remuneration was low; most saw their Fellowships as an avenue to rich ecclesiastical livings. Academic life was about promotion, promotion about religion

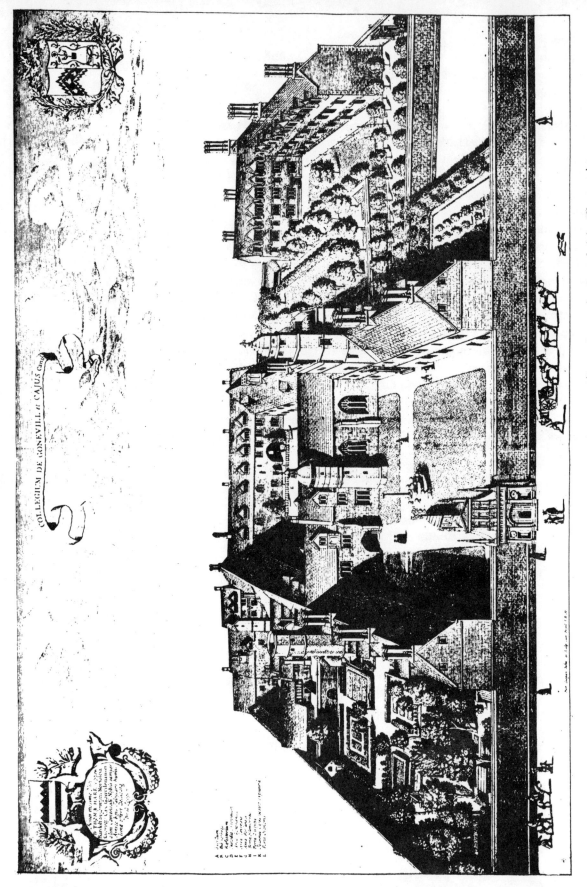

Gonville and Caius College at the turn of the 17th century (from Loggan's *Cantabrigia Illustrata*)

and politics. Cambridge adopted the general latitudinarianism of the times, eschewing discussion of 'petty' doctrinal points. Political connections were vital. The university was a Tory stronghold until 1734, St John's harbouring many non-juror Fellows. This changed under the Chancellorship of the great Whig power-broker, the Duke of Newcastle. He used his power at Cambridge to reward followers with positions there, and promoted Whig interests, interfering with college elections to do so.

Some efforts were made to tackle the prevailing laxity. In the 1770s there were campaigns to establish annual examinations in law, history, classics, and natural sciences. These failed, as did a struggle to admit Dissenters to degrees. Some material improvements were made. The Botanic Gardens were established, the University Library extended and a new range built at Emmanuel. University members participated in demands for parliamentary reform, an end to the American War, and, above all, the abolition of the slave trade. Thomas Clarkson, a son of Wisbech, became the leading English proponent of abolition, from his Cambridge study. Coleridge won a Browne Medal for a Greek Ode on the topic. The outbreak of the French Revolution caused the foundation of several Debating Clubs. These signs of radicalism were, however, ruthlessly suppressed by Isaac Milner, President of Queens' and an arch-Tory. Milner actively persecuted Liberal dons, one chief sufferer being William Frend of Jesus. Dissenters and Whigs fell silent. Coleridge showed his feelings by burning the slogan 'Liberty, Equality and Fraternity' on to his college lawn. It was a rare protest. Cambridge in 1800 was intellectually moribund, and politically repressive.

Resurrection

The years between 1800 and 1870 saw a rebirth in university life. The greatest change was in numbers. From 150 freshmen a year, the annual intake rose to 450 by 1850, and to 800 freshmen 20 years later. This resulted in much new building, and King's, Trinity, Peterhouse, Corpus Christi, and St John's all erected new wings, many in fashionable neo-Gothic style. The century symbolically began with a new foundation, the first in over 200 years. Downing College was established under the will of Sir George Downing of Gamlingay. His grand plans had to be scaled down in practice, and the college did not open until 1821, but it remained a new start.

The growth in numbers was accompanied by changes in the behaviour of the dons. Sloth and drunkenness among Fellows remained common into Victorian times. Thereafter, a general spirit of endeavour—if not sobriety—developed. Education became a serious

Arms of Downing College

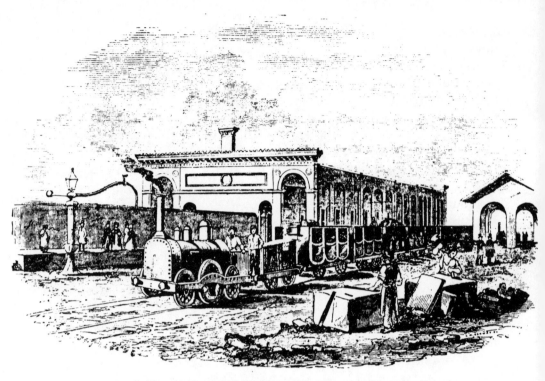

Cambridge Station in 1845. (From *The Illustrated London News*)

business, a search after truth and a training for life. The Victorian ideal was the 'liberal education', a broad-based curriculum designed to produce the perfect man, at home in library, laboratory, and playing-field. The domination of mathematics was increasingly criticised. A Classics Tripos was introduced in 1822, and a 'Previous Examination' requiring Greek and Latin. These, however, remained adjuncts to the main, mathematical examinations. It was still an age of mathematicians: Peacock, Herschel, Babbage, de Morgan, Stokes, and Cayley. Advances elsewhere relied mainly on application of mathematical techniques: Airy and Adams in astronomy; Green, Kelvin, and Maxwell in physics. Classics was a 'soft option', overwhelmingly geared to grammar and textual criticism at the expense of historical or philosophical content. The narrow-based curriculum was attacked in parliament, with attempts at reform in the 1830s and 1840s. Prince Albert eventually precipitated change, as Chancellor after 1847. New Tripos examinations were established in 'Moral Sciences' and 'Natural Philosophy'. A Royal Commission recommended boards of study for all major subjects, new honours courses in modern languages, and civil engineering, and an increase in the number of professorships—all to be financed by the colleges. University government was streamlined. New chairs were founded in archaeology, sanskrit, zoology, mechanics, Anglo-Saxon,

110

ecclesiastical history and political economy. Their remuneration, however, was minimal, giving little incentive for vigorous teaching courses. Only in 1861 did the Tripos examinations in moral sciences and natural philosophy acquire first degree status. Theology likewise had to wait until 1874, before the examination established for it two decades before brought a degree.

This was the period of Darwin. The university produced many great names, in various fields: statesmen like Lord Melbourne, Lord Palmerston, and Stratford Canning; literary figures like Byron, Thackeray and Tennyson all cut their teeth here. The union society was founded as a political debating club in 1815, despite strong official disapproval. The Apostles, a group of radical intellectuals, added to undergraduate thought in the 1830s and 1840s. Darwin belonged to neither. His student years were frivolous, spent riding, shooting and gambling; yet somewhere he gained the enquiring mind that made him the outstanding figure of Victorian science. He was the greatest vindication of the liberal ideal.

New scholarship notwithstanding, undergraduate life remained generally idle. Leslie Stephen delivered a breathtaking broadside at such 'Varmints' in the *Pall Mall Gazette*. 'A young Englishman at a University is remarkably like a young Englishman anywhere else . . . full of animal spirits, a thoroughly good fellow, and intensely and incredibly ignorant.' Even in 1870, ordinary degrees exceeded honours by 10 per cent —and the ordinary examinations were of notoriously low standards. The greatest change in student life was not so much in study as in sports. These were actively encouraged under the liberal ideal, and followed the emphasis on sport evident in public schools. Rowing came to Cambridge in the 1820s, with Boat Clubs, the Bumps, and the Boat Race. Cricket began at the Fenners ground, rapidly becoming the second university sport. Racquets, rugby and football gained popularity, and the first agreed rules for Association Football were developed in Cambridge. Afternoon exercise was expected, like chapel attendance on Sundays. For many, 'afternoons' became the whole day. Even this, however, began to change. The abolition of many closed scholarships and the old divisions of pensioners, sizars, etc., in mid-century made all students nominally equal, and all had to take an examination of some kind to graduate. The university was slowly assuming a modern shape.

A Modern University? (1870–1900)

Modernisation quickened after 1870, the greatest change being financial. Cambridge education previously had depended upon the colleges. Tuition was carried out within each college, by academics expected to be jacks of all trades. Lecturing and research suffered. Subjects requiring expensive and bulky equipment could not be taught efficiently at collegiate level. A Royal Commission in 1873 therefore proposed financing education by grants, from the different colleges to university boards of study (later, faculties). These became responsible for teaching. College Fellowships were linked to university lectureships, in specialised subjects.

This technical change made possible the construction of new university buildings after 1880. The New Museum site was expanded to include buildings for engineering and several sciences, sprawling across Downing Street into the old Botanic Gardens (now removed to Station Corner). The Cavendish Laboratories acquired the latest equipment, and an enviable research reputation.

Carving from Christ's College (18th century)

Material expansion was matched by growth in the number of subjects taught. Lecturing staff increased in number by 30 per cent., and new chairs were created across the range of the sciences and arts. History acquired its own Tripos in 1875, followed quickly by Semitic, Indian, medieval and modern languages. Faculties quickly threw up eminent scholars. Physicists like Rutherford and Thomson (of X-ray fame) competed for acclaim with the geneticist Bateson, zoologists Newton and Balfour. Medicine flourished under Paget and Foster, mathematics maintaining its Cambridge tradition with Bertrand Russell and A. N. Whitehead. History owes much to Seeley and Maitland, classics to Jebb, Jackson, and A. E. Housman. Oriental languages possessed two international scholars in W. R. Smith and E. G. Browne. Quiller-Couch ('Q') transformed the English faculty after 1912. A Board of Extra-Mural Studies was established in 1873, for the education of students outside the Cambridge area. Existing Oxford and Cambridge school examination systems were united, and schoolchildren throughout England sat papers produced by the premier universities.

The religious and emotional constraints on university life simultaneously loosened with the decision to admit Dissenters to degrees and Fellowships, and to permit dons to marry. Many criticised the latter decision, fearing the breakdown of communal, collegiate life, but the benefits were many. A man might at last see academia as a permanent career, rather than a staging-post to something else.

It was in its attitude to women students that the university displayed its worst colours. Lack of female education had become a scandal that a few were beginning to recognise. One result was the establishment of women's 'colleges'—for they were not recognised as such—at Cambridge. Girton was founded in 1869, the college itself being constructed far enough from the city to preserve the reputation

112

39. One of the most photographed views in Cambridge: Great Court, Trinity, looking north east to the chapel and gatehouse. The fountain is a spectacular late-Elizabethan structure.

40. The Cloister Court at Queen's College, Cambridge, built in the 15th century. It makes an ideal setting for Shakespearian and other Tudor plays performed here in the Easter Term.

41. Christopher Wren's magnificent Library at Trinity was begun in 1676 and completed in 1690. Over 150 ft. long, it is built of Ketton stone in a classical, Tuscan style.

42. The most famous view in Cambridge: King's College Chapel, Clare College and the Cam from the Backs. A maze of wharves, warehouses and narrow lanes stood east of the Can in the early Middle Ages.

43. The screen, organ and roof of King's College Chapel make this one of the most inspiring interiors in England, a more-than-fitting memorial to the College's unfortunate founder, Henry VI.

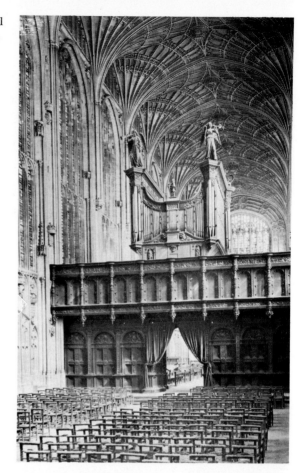

44. A detail from the organ screen in King's College, Cambridge. Note the maze of Tudor symbols: roses, portcullises and inter-laced initials. Pevsner calls the chapel screen 'the purest work in the Early Renaissance style in England'.

45. The gatehouse of St John's College, Cambridge is 16th century, standing three storeys high. The heraldic animals are known as yales—goats' heads, antelopes' bodies and elephants' tails.

46. A distant view over Linton Village College shortly after its construction in 1937. The Village Colleges are Cambridgeshire's own unique contribution to the history of modern education in Britain.

of its students! It was soon followed by Newnham, situated pragmatically close to the centre, but across the river. The academic establishment and male undergraduates combined ferociously to resist the women's demands for degrees. Campaigns in 1888 and 1897 failed amid hysterical chauvinism,

THE UNIVERSITY FOR·THE UNDERGRADUATE
Maintain the Integrity of Cambridge
Beware of the Thin Edge of the Wedge
DOWN WITH WOMEN'S DEGREES
DOWN WITH THE FADDISTS

screamed one poster. The Union Society rejected the change by 1,000 to 138 votes. Female effigies were hung over Trinity; Caius College was graced with a banner proclaiming: 'Get you to Girton, Beatrice, get you to Newnham: here is no place for maids'. Assumptions of male superiority were dented when a Newnham student taking the same mathematics examinations scored higher than the First Wrangler. The victory, however, was moral—the defeat actual.

THE CITY

Rutland and Reform

Cambridge politics in the 18th and 19th centuries was generally unedifying: a mixture of influence, corruption and reaction.

The first conflict came in the brief reign of James II. While imposing Catholics upon the university, James also strove to extend his control over the city through a 'more precise' charter. This allowed the crown to dismiss any official. A drastic purge, involving almost the whole Corporation from the mayor downwards, resulted. The new, nominated Corporation created 150 freemen to dominate the electorate, and the revolution of 1688 came none too soon for the borough's peace and independence. For 20 years, internecine electoral battles between Whigs and Tories split Cambridge into rival factions, competing with words and wallets. The Tories' national defeat after 1714 and Whig supremacy created political torpor in the city, though it was not until 1741 that Cambridge entered the Whig camp. Tory feelings were maintained by the city's first newspaper, *The Cambridge Journal,* founded in 1744. Staunchly patriotic, Anglican and Tory, it condemned the '45 Rebellion with unashamed obloquy: 'NO PRETENDER, NO SLAVERY, NO POPERY. NO FRENCH INFLUENCE, NO ARBITRARY POWER'. Whig voters were 'filthy Owls of Prey, who dread the Light'. Its bias and dullness allowed a rival, *The Chronicle,* to develop after 1762: a middle-of-the-road

113

paper, supporting the government and local M.P., a client of Hardwicke. The Wimpole interest dominated in Cambridge, as in the shire, though later the situation was to change.

Cambridge Corporation had always contained several Dissenters, despite Test and Corporation Acts. The Purchas family had been aldermen and mayors over successive generations. In the 1770s, demands for parliamentary reform, an end to the American Wars, and freedom of conscience were echoed locally by Alderman Tunwell and his followers. A meeting in 1780 addressed by the radical, John Wilkes, drew an enormous crowd. By this time, the Tory Rutlands were also dabbling in city politics—and it was their influence which eventually prevailed. A central figure in this was the local merchant and banker, John Mortlock III. Mortlock began his career on the reform ticket, but soon became a major political fixer. He used wealth to buy support, and power to swell his purse. In 1784 he was M.P. for Cambridge, backed by the Rutlands. Three years later, he sold his interest to the arch-Rutlandite, William Pitt, for a sinecure worth £1,000 per annum. Seventy-three new freemen were created, to ensure the dominance of the Rutlands over the parliamentary seat and of Mortlock over the Corporation. Mortlock was mayor of Cambridge 13 times in the following two decades.

This Tory domination contrasted strongly with the radical feelings of many inhabitants. The French Revolution was greeted with enthusiasm. Cambridge had its own radical paper, *The Intelligencer,* distributed throughout Britain under its energetic editor, Benjamin Fowler. It worked closely with the city's Constitutional Society, attacking slavery, borough corruption, the French Wars, and the refusal of parliament to reform itself or grant Catholic emancipation. Fowler was harassed by the local Corporation and national government, and imprisoned in Newgate in 1799, on a trumped-up libel charge.

The passing of the Napoleonic Wars and Mortlock brought new pressures. An independent press was created, and elections contested in 1819-20. These, however, only confirmed the grip of Tories and their 118 non-resident voting freemen on the parliamentary seat and Corporation. Cambridge had become a pocket borough. Charities were allowed to lapse, proceeds channelled into the public purse. City property was sold to Corporation members and friends at nominal sums. Thrice as much money was spent on Corporation dinners at the Rutland Club as on public works. *The Times* recorded its sober judgement in 1833:

> Probably no judicial investigation ever brought to light more shameless profligacy or more inveterate dishonesty, more bare-faced venality in politics, a more heartless disregard of the claims of the poor, in the

114

perversion of the funds left for their benefit, a more degrading subserviency to the views of the rich, a more insatiable cupidity in the corporate officers to enrich themselves with the corporate property, or a more entire neglect of their duties and functions as magistrates.

The 1832 Reform Act and Municipal Reform Act three years later destroyed this picture. Two Liberals were elected to parliament, and the Rutland interest banished from the Corporation. The Reform Act ensured an unrepresentative but sizeable electorate of about 1600, which doubled in 1867. Liberals and Tories alternately dominated Cambridge politics, neither establishing complete control. Corruption remained common, and Tories were unseated in 1853 and 1865 for purchasing votes with beer. By 1886, however, the electorate was over 6,000, and corruption much less visible. The city was also stabilising politically, in the Tory interest.

The Life of the Poor

Cambridge's population increased from 9,000 in 1801 to almost 40,000 a century later. The increase in the size of the university played some part, as did the immigration of unemployed farmhands seeking work. Most of the explosion, however, came from a soaring birth rate and declining mortality. One result was an enormous expansion in the city boundaries. The centre was already densely settled. In practice, 95 per cent. of the expansion lay east and south-east, in the parish of St Andrew the Less—in the Kite, Barnwell, and Romsey areas. The other main settlement was New Town, between Lensfield Road and Hills Road. This new housing rose without public planning or control. Overcrowding was a fact of life; 18 per cent. of the population lived in courts, yards, and alleyways. An 1849 report considered 'the conditions . . . so wretched as to be a disgrace on civilisation; it is next to impossible for the inhabitants to be healthy, moral, decent or honest'. Barnwell acquired an appalling reputation for theft, prostitution and violent crime. Church missions were despatched to the area, with philanthropic associations competing to help. One of the worst districts, ironically, was 'The Garden of Eden'—once a small field, now divided into Eden Street, Adam and Eve Street, and Paradise Row.

Accommodation was mainly in two-storey terraced houses with brick and slate roofs, still standing today in large areas of Cambridge. Most were constructed by small builders on borrowed capital; the desire for quick profit prevented the provision of sanitation, paving or other facilities. Only in superior, middle-class streets interspersed with the slums—Brookside, Maid's Causeway, Warkworth Street—were attempts made to provide more than a space to live. Matters of public health lay entirely with the Corporation, which was slow to meet the challenge. Councillors and aldermen argued that it was not their responsibility, citing a Parliamentary Act of 1544. An Improvement Commission was established in 1788 to pave, light and cleanse Cambridge. Their work saw sterling progress in central Cambridge, but their power and finance was insufficient to tackle the new suburbs. Typhoid outbreaks were common, many inhabitants being a quarter of a mile from clean water supplies. Public health improved only slowly. Fresh-water wells were opened at Cherry Hinton in 1855, and main drainage was gradually extended throughout Cambridge. The powers of the Improvement Commission and Corporation were merged in 1875, with good results. By 1900, a system of deep sewers covered the city, the outfall lying away from the city centre.

Plan of Cambridge Workhouse

Addenbrookes Hospital was founded in the 1760s, under the will of a Fellow of St Catharine's. It expanded rapidly in size during the 19th century despite chronic financial difficulties. By 1900, the hospital handled 1,300 patients a year, four times the number of a century before. New wards were built in 1878, a dormitory five years later, and an out-patients department and nurses' accommodation in 1895. The apothecary, matron and four nurses of 1767 had turned into four resident doctors, 40 nurses, six visiting physicians and surgeons from the university—Fellows in medicine using Addenbrookes as a teaching hospital.

Education simultaneously progressed. The Quakers set up the first New Free School in Jesus Lane in 1808. Charity schools and state funding here as in Cambridgeshire brought free, compulsory education to all by 1880. The establishment of a public library in 1885, again largely due to the Quakers, catered for the minds of adult townsfolk. Security was provided by the institution of the police, in the middle of the century.

The poverty and squalor of living conditions should not be overlooked. Even in the early 19th century, however, the poor had their consolations. Many were helped by religion, particularly by the Dissenting churches and Baptists establishing a hold on the minds of the poor in the 18th century which they were never completely to lose. For others, there were always occasional times of merriment. Midsummer Fair was a traditional time of revelry. Other celebrations were for specific events. The end of the Napoleonic Wars and the visit of Blucher was made an occasion of raucous joy. Even this was exceeded in 1838 during the Coronation of Queen Victoria. Then, 14,000 poor inhabitants of the city dined on Parker's Piece, on 60 tables radiating from the centre like the spokes of a wheel. There was

116

cold meat and pickles, bread, plum pudding, and beer. Over 1,000 joints and 1,600 puddings were consumed. Midsummer Common housed rustic sports—donkey races, grinning competitions, biscuit bolting for the children, swings and roundabouts. A balloon ascent and fireworks capped the day, making the Coronation indeed a time to remember. Such festivities were rare, but much appreciated!

Transport and Trade

Cambridge's economic heart in the 18th century was Stourbridge Fair. Defoe described it as the biggest in the world. An enormous variety of textile products (silk, linen, wool) vied for attention with the goods of ironmongers, tobacconists, leatherworkers, perfumers, cabinet-makers, glass-blowers, toy manufacturers, and picture sellers. There was a book auction for the university. The greatest trade was in hops and cloth. Defoe talks of £10,000 deals, and at one Fair £60,000 worth of wool was sold from Lincolnshire alone. The Fair lasted four weeks, on the Common beside the river. Booths were arranged in 'streets'—Garlick Row, Cheapside, Cork Row, Duddery. Merchants came from throughout Britain and Continental ports from Danzig to Brest.

By 1800, the Fair was clearly declining. Considerable business was still done, but the number of special coaches from London had shrunk from 60 to ten. By 1830, the Fair lasted only a fortnight, and 10 years later was a single row of stalls. In the Victorian period its popularity was eclipsed. By 1897, it lasted three days only, and only the horse sale showed economic vitality. The Fair was last proclaimed in 1933, to an audience of three. Cambridge's other fairs—Garlic and Midsummer—had also declined. The former, always small, ceased in 1808. Midsummer Fair, once a miniature Stourbridge with pots, china, millinery and pictures as the main goods became a pleasure fair only, and survives today.

The early greatness and later decline of these fairs rested on transport and communications. Cambridge's strategic position at the head of the fenland river system, with good land routes to London, East Anglia and the East Midlands ironically improved with dredging in the Cam, enabling barges to reach the city centre. Wharves, warehouses and workshops jostled for room with colleges and boarding-inns. A planned canal to Bishop's Stortford and London never materialised, but the development of turnpike roads and fast stage-coaches for passenger traffic eased communication to other parts of England. The London coaches, taking 6½ hours, were especially good. Names like *Wellington, Hero, Regulator* and *Defiant* competed for custom down

117

the Great North Road. Unfortunately, the development of better road and canal communications throughout England removed much of Cambridge's strategic advantage, precipitating her decline. The decisive factor, however, was the coming of the railways. The first line reached the city in 1845, as part of a through London–Norwich route operated by the Eastern Counties (later Great Eastern) Railway. This followed 13 frustrating years of schemes which would at various times have linked Cambridge with York, Derby, Manchester, and the Midlands. The station was impressively classical, a single long platform accommodating up and down trains. A second wooden platform was abandoned in 1875. The initial daily service provided seven through trains, the fastest taking just under two hours to reach Shoreditch at a first-class single fare of 10s. 6d.—a week's wages for a labourer! Technological advance reduced the journey to 1¼ hours by 1883, from which odd minutes have been whittled in the 20th century.

The London–Norwich route was the first of several through Cambridge. The Great Northern Railway made persistent attempts to gain its own access via Hitchin and Royston. Competition between the two railways ended in a settlement, the G.N.R. obtaining a link to Cambridge on to its King's Cross line. An attempt to provide a London–Newmarket line via Great Chesteford in 1847 failed despite support from Rutland and the Jockey Club; this left Cambridge as the only link to the races, Ipswich and Suffolk stations. Other towns were connected to the city by branch lines: St Ives and Peterborough in 1847, Bedford and Oxford in 1862, Colchester and Haverhill in 1865, Kettering a year later. The extension of the main line to Ely and King's Lynn finally destroyed Stourbridge Fair, and the fenland trading system. The barges and wharves vanished; Cambridge ceased to be an inland port.

This did not so much destroy as alter the pattern of city life, and Cambridge became a minor industrial centre and market town of the area. It was a banking centre, too. Above all, it served the university. The colleges stimulated every branch of trade, from building, victualling, printing, and general retailing to domestic service. Slums notwithstanding, Cambridge to the visitor appeared a bustling, prosperous place. Its own internal transportation network developed rapidly. Trams, buses and the ubiquitous bicycle replaced horses and carriages. The railways brought the rural middle classes into town for shopping. Cambridge had lost a commercial empire, but found an acceptable role.

Town and Gown

This account has separated city and university. In fact, Cambridge and its colleges were mutually dependent. In economic life, the

118

university was a dominating force, using its position to prevent the development of major industries. Politically, dons influenced city life. Several 19th-century M.P.s were academics, including the redoubtable Reform Whig, George Pryme. Others became councillors, aldermen and mayors. In 1889, the university was allowed to elect six councillors and two aldermen to the Council in its own right, in effect becoming two city wards.

A Proctor in full robes

The university retained wide powers in areas normally controlled by local Corporations. It licensed all alehouses, markets and fairs, as well as theatrical and other entertainments. It had jurisdiction over trade, including weights and measures. Tradesmen were obliged to inform colleges of all undergraduate debts, on pain of blacklisting. City and university nominally controlled law and order jointly, but the absence of an effective watchman system left early policing to university proctors. These used their rights to supervise undergraduate morality to arrest 'loose women' found with students on the streets. The isolation of the railway station from the city was ordained by the university, fearful of its impact on student life. Trains were policed by a special university force and undergraduates could be questioned.

The Corporation resisted these powers, gradually winning concessions in the 19th century. The licensing power over theatres was shared after 1856, and abandoned entirely in the 1890s. The mayor's oath to maintain university privileges was likewise rescinded in 1856. Other casualties were the loss of the vice-chancellor's authority over weights and measures, alehouses and victualling. University and College property became rated, contributing to the public funds. Proctorial powers of policing and discipline, however, remained until the 1890s, Cambridge women being the main sufferers. The 'Spinning House' jail became a hated symbol of university power, containing real and supposed prostitutes convicted before university courts without proper judicial procedures. The controversy culminated after the escape of Jane Elsden from the Spinning House, and her subsequent recapture. Cambridge newspapers were on Elsden's side, and the university was forced to concede jurisdiction to the borough magistrates.

This public bickering was echoed by inveterate hostility on a personal level. Student-bashing remains an unwelcome fact of Cambridge life. In the 18th century, undergraduates and town ruffians were equally fearsome, committing assaults on the unwary and upon each other. Undergraduates sometimes rioted against unpopular personalities within the university; one Senior Proctor in 1829 precipitated a demonstration by his strict exercise of discipline. Sometimes, it was specifically a town/gown affair. John Death, mayor of Cambridge in 1875, used police to curb the students' violence. In retaliation undergraduates burned him in effigy, disrupted a concert at which he was present, and attacked shops and buildings in the city centre. Townsfolk equally protested with missiles and fists during disputes over university privileges. Stourbridge Fair became a particular time of violence. The lives of the 'young gentlemen' and Cambridge youths were mutually incomprehensible. Only in our own century has their difference lessened, and some of the aggression ceased.

THE TWENTIETH CENTURY

The changes visible in the 19th century have continued and accelerated into our own times. The university has become far more open and democratic. In 1900, colleges remained institutions for the nobility and professional classes. The extension of the university system and introduction of compulsory secondary education has increased the size and altered the nature of the student population. Most students today come from the middle and occasionally working classes, and have got to Cambridge through scholastic merit. The aristocratic remnant remain powerful in student life, but do not determine the average undergraduate lifestyle. This is particularly true in the many new colleges. The nature of education has changed.Women have finally been admitted to degrees and segregation of colleges by sex has increasingly been broken down. New subjects have entered the curriculum. Research for the Ph.D. has become the first step towards an academic career. The importance of the university within British public life remains high; Cambridge graduates sally forth to take 'Glittering Prizes' in different fields, despite greater competition.

The city has, to some extent, also changed its role. The university remains its most important employer, determining much of its economic life. Industries like Pye Telecom have, however, provided other sources of work, as have the chemical giants south of the city. Many undertakings, like the Science Park at Milton, are direct attempts to exploit the researches of scientists within the university. The borough —it became officially what it had always been, a city, in 1951— continued to expand, with dormitory villages at Coton, the Shelfords and Fulbourn. The improvement of living conditions and public facilities in the 20th century is rather a part of the general history of Britain, than that specifically of Cambridge, but has left us almost unable to comprehend the life of our predecessors only a century ago. *Autres temps, autres moeurs.*

In 1964, Cambridgeshire and the Isle of Ely were formally merged into the new county of Cambridge and the Isle. Ten years later, the county expanded again to take in Huntingdonshire and the Soke of Peterborough. This book has therefore been the history of an area not defined as a county except for one decade. Historically, however, southern Cambridgeshire and the Isle have had many links. Today, these lines are formalised in the greater shire.

Select Bibliography

The following books were of particular use to me in compiling this history, and deserve exploration by the serious reader

Allen, C. J., *The Great Eastern Railway* 1955).
Allen, C. J., *The London and North Eastern Railway* (1974).
Astbury, J., *The Black Fens.*
Barrett, W. H., *A Fenman's Story.*
Bloom, A., *The Farm in the Fen* (1945).
British Association for the Advancement of Science, *The Cambridge Region* (1965).
Cambridgeshire County Council, *Riot and Be Hanged* (1971).
Chamberlain, M., *Fenwomen* (1976).
Darby, H. C., *et al, Early Cambridgeshire* (1979).
Darby, H. C., *The Draining of the Fens* (1956).
Darby, H. C., *The Medieval Fenland* (1973).
Fellows, R. B., *Railways to Cambridge Actual and Proposed* (1976).
Fox, C. F., *Archaeology of the Cambridge Region* (1936 edn.).
Gooch, W., *General View of the Agriculture of Cambridgeshire* (1813).
Gray, A. B., *Some Old Industries of Cambridge* (1918).
Grove, R., *Cambridgeshire Coprolite Mining Rush* (1975).
Hampson, W. M., *The Treatment of Poverty in Cambridgeshire* (1934).
Individual Histories of Colleges.
Lethbridge, T. C., *Gogmagog* (1954).
Lobel, M. D., *Cambridge* (1974).
Lysons, D., *Magna Britannia: Cambridge* (1797).
Marshall, D., *Fenland Chronicle.*
Palmer, W. M., *Cambridge Castle* (1976).
Parker, R., *The Common Stream* (1975).
Peacock, A. J., *Bread or Blood.*
Pevsner, N., *The Buildings of England: Cambridgeshire* (1972).
Porter, E., *Cambridge Stage Coaches.*
Porter, E., *Cambridgeshire Customs and Folklore* (1969).
Porter, E., *The River Trade of Old Cambridgeshire.*
Ravensdale, J., *Liable to Floods* (1974).
Reaney, P. H., *Place Names of Cambridgeshire* (1943).
Reeves, F. A., *Victorian and Edwardian Cambridge* (1971).

Royal Commission on Ancient and Historic Monuments, Cambridge-
    shire Vols. I and II; Cambridge Vols. I and II.
Spufford, M., *Contrasting Communities* (1974).
Swingle, S., *Cambridge Street Tramways* (1972).
Taylor, C. C., *The Making of the Cambridgeshire Landscape.*
Vancouver, G., *General View of the Agriculture in Cambridgeshire* (1794).
Victoria County History of Cambridgeshire.
Wilson, J. K., *Fenland Barge Traffic* (1972).

Index

Edward VI, 55
Edward the Elder, 34, 35
Elizabeth I, 56
Elm, 63
Elsworth, 61
Eltisley, 60
Ely, 13, 24, 29, 31, 33, 35, 36, 39, 40,
    41, 42, 60, 62, 63, 64, 65, 70, 71,
    77, 82, 87, 97, 100, 104, 118
Emmanuel College, 58, 69-70, 109
'Epona', 21
Erasmus, 54
Ermine Street, 24, 97
Ethelred, 34, 35
Ethelreda (Saint), 33, 36
Exning, 31, 104

Felix (Saint), 33
Feltwell, 79
Fen Drayton, 26
Fen Ditton, 40, 41, 60
Field Patterns, 34, 61
Fiennes, Celia, 82
Fisher, 52, 54
Flaggrass, 27
Fordham, 41
Fowler, Benjamin, 114
Fowlmere, 18
Fulbourn, 120
Fursa (Saint), 33

Gamlingay, 93, 109
Garlic Fair, 117
Geoffrey de Mandeville, 39
Gervase of Tilbury, 21
Girton College, 112
Girton Village, 14, 27, 30, 31, 35
Godmanchester, 24
Gogmagog, 21
Gonville and Caius, 51, 58, 69, 108,
    113
Gooch, William, 91
Grantchester, 17, 25, 30
Great Abington, 65
Great Chesterford, 22, 24
Great Ouse, 25, 34, 77, 79, 82, 85, 87,
    89
Great St Mary's, 52, 58, 69
Great Shelford, 60, 63, 92, 120
Grime's Graves, 15
Grunty Fen, 16
Guilden Morden, 20, 28, 60, 100
Guyhirn, 77, 79, 104
Gyrwe, 31, 33

Haddenham, 82
Hadrian, 26
Hadstock, 35
Hardwicke, Earls of, 93ff
Harlton, 11
Harston, 13
Haslingfield, 11, 17, 30, 66

Hauxton, 17, 28, 42
Henry I, 39
Henry VI, 53
Henry VII, 66, 77
Henry VIII, 55, 65
Hereward the Wake, 36-7
Heydon Ditch, 31
Hildersham, 91
Hilgay, 103
Histon, 92
Horningsea, 27
Horseheath, 24, 26, 60, 103

Iceni, 18, 22
Icknield Way, 13, 15, 24, 33, 92, 97
Isleham, 42, 63

James I, 69, 77
James II, 113
John, King, 39-40
Jesus College, 74, 109

Kennett, 14
Kinderley, Charles, 83
King's College, 53, 74, 109
King's Ditch, 58
King's Hall, 51, 55
King's Lynn, 25, 47, 77, 84, 85, 118
Kingston, 11, 47, 60, 92
Kirkling, 66, 97
Knapwell, 39

Landbeach, 67
Landwade, 27
Lark, River, 82, 85
Latimer, Hugh, 54, 55
Laud, Archbishop, 69ff
Lethbridge, T. C., 21
Leverington, 43, 63, 66
Liber Eliensis, 43
Linton, 17, 26, 30, 46, 47, 68, 71, 97,
    102
Litlington, 27
Little Abington, 65
Little Germany, 54
Little Gransden, 92
Littleport, 25, 43, 97, 100ff
Little Ouse, 47, 82, 85
Little Shelford, 92
Longstowe, 62, 63
Langthorpe, 22

Madingley, 60, 66, 93
Magdalene College, 54, 74
Manea, 26
March, 13, 22, 26, 63, 103
Mare Way, 11
Mary Tudor, 55, 65
Melbourn, 15, 70, 95, 96
Meldreth, 92
Mercia, 31
Michaelhouse, 51, 52, 55